Blake's 7

Season Four Guide

OTHER VIEWER'S GUIDE BOOKS BY THE SAME AUTHOR

Blake's 7 Season One Guide
Blake's 7 Season Two Guide
Blake's 7 Season Three Guide

Doctor Who: The Fifth Doctor Viewer's Guide

Gerry & Sylvia Anderson's UFO. Series Guide, Volume One: The Beginning: Straker and Foster

Gerry and Sylvia Anderson's UFO. Series Guide, Volume Two: Straker's Private Life

Gerry & Sylvia Anderson's UFO. Series Guide, Volume Three: Straker versus the Aliens

Lost in Space Original Series Guide

Sapphire & Steel Viewer's Guide

Space:1999 Year One Viewer's Guide

Space: 1999 Year Two Viewer's Guide Second Edition

Space:1999 Complete Series Viewer's Guide: Collector's Edition

The Quatermass Experiment and its Legacy: The Birth of BBC Science Fiction

The Tomorrow People: Original Series Guide

The Tomorrow People Original Series Guide: Expanded Second Edition

**OTHER FICTION
BY THE SAME AUTHOR**

Damon Dark: Biodome

Lethbridge-Stewart: The New Unusual
by Adrian Sherlock and Andy Frankham-Allen

Sherlock Holmes: Time Detective: The Complete Adventures Collection

Aiden's Powers: The Boy Who Defends the Earth: Volume 1

Blake's 7

Season Four Guide

ADRIAN SHERLOCK

2024

Copyright © 2024 Adrian Sherlock

This book is a work of journalism. It is published under fair comment and fair use laws, including creative commons laws. Every reasonable effort has been made by the author to avoid copyright infringement. All quotes and references to intellectual property are done so for the sake of review, criticism, and analysis. No copyright infringement is intended.

All Rights Reserved. This book or any portion thereof may not be reproduced or used in any manner whatsoever without the prior written permission of the copyright owner except for the use of brief quotations in a book review.

Cover art by Kevin Langille

"Thank you" illustration by Aiden Sherlock

First printing, 2024

DEDICATED TO

Michael Keating

SEASON FOUR

(1981)

THE AUTHOR WISHES TO THANK

NEIL SHEARER AND TONY MURRAY

BRENDAN HARRISON, PAUL FOSTER

AND KEVIN POWELL

AND MEMBERS OF

THE ONLINE BLAKE'S 7

FAN COMMUNITY

CAST LIST

Avon - Paul Darrow

Vila - Michael Keating

Tarrant - Steven Pacey

Dayna - Josette Simon

Soolin - Glynis Barber

Orac/Slave - Peter Tuddenham

RECURRING CAST

Servalan - Jacqueline Pearce

Blake - Gareth Thomas

GUEST CAST

Dorian - Geoffrey Burridge

The Creature - Rob Middleton

Gunn Sar - Dicken Ashworth

Pella - Juliet Hammond Hill

Leitz - Malcolm Stoddard

Colonel Quute - Christopher Neame

Dr. Plaxton - Barbara Shelley

Atlan - Damien Thomas

Justin - Peter Byrne

Captain - William Lindsay

Muller - John Westbrook

Vena - Lynda Bellingham

Technician - Douglas Fielding

Android - Nick Joseph

Verlis - Betty Marsden

Nebrox - Richard Hurndall

Piri - Caroline Holdaway

Cancer - John Wyman

Benos - Peter Attard

Tok - Adam Blackwood

Belkov - Stratford Johns

Gerren - David Neal

Guard - James Harvey

Gambit - Rosalind Bailey

Reeve - Stephen Yardley

Chasgo - Daniel Hill

Keiller - Roy Kinnear

Slaten - Anthony Brown

Egrorian - John Savident

Pinder - Larry Noble

Zukan - Roy Boyd

Zeeona - Bobbie Brown

Finn - Dean Harris

Boorva - Simon Merrick

Deva - David Collings

Arlen - Sasha Mitchell

FOREWORD

Welcome, fellow member of the galactic rebellion, to the fourth volume of the *Blake's 7 Viewer's Guide*!

Season three of *Blake's 7* had ended with the destruction of the beloved starship Liberator, that iconic vessel which had first lit the spark of imagination in Roj Blake with its promise of the power to strike back against tyranny, while igniting a desire for freedom in Kerr Avon.

Often cited by *Blake's 7* fans as 'the most beautiful ship in space', it was truly one of the most iconic and photogenic craft ever brought to the screen, its alien origins only adding to its appeal, bringing mystique to the aesthetics.

The Liberator had come mysteriously from the universe, like a gift from the unknown, setting Blake and his friends free from their plight aboard the prison-ship London.

No longer doomed to condemnation for life on the sinister Cygnus Alpha, they were empowered by this unexpected bounty from beyond. It was not merely the craft to liberate the oppressed inhabitants of the galaxy; it was the tool of their personal liberation, as well.

Thus, it was somehow appropriate then that the mysterious depths of outer space and the universe had destroyed the Liberator with a cloud of unknown alien enzymes. Motiveless, wordless, enigmatic micro-organisms from the darkness of the void had laid waste to the ship and robbed our heroes of all the empowerment and hope that it embodied.

It was almost as if the same universe which had given them the miraculous starship was now reclaiming it. The *Blake's 7* universe 'giveth' and 'taketh away' in equal measure, as if some even-handed cosmic God wanted to keep things 'fair'.

In this way it is fitting that it was not Earth's totalitarian Federation that had finally brought down the mighty starship Liberator. That would have been too vindicating for the bad side of the human race, too validating for the power of the oppressor.

This sense of the mysterious universe giving and taking in equal measure suggested there was a certain balance, too, a certain sense of the Yin and the Yang, life and death or, perhaps, the light and the dark.

In much more practical terms, for the viewing audience and the producers of the series, this loss of the Liberator impacted the look, style and feel of the series.

Gone were the strange, transparent weapons which were pointed like a flashlight and killed with an unseen power discharged from an illuminated rod. Gone, too, was the semi-organic design and implied depths of the vast and moody Liberator interior.

In its place was a new vessel, a spaceship built by humans. Fully lit, the set for the inside of the Scorpio had none of the mood, none of the deep shadows, and none of the mystery of the Liberator.

The new handguns which came with the Scorpio, although an impressive and sturdy piece of prop-work, look depressingly familiar in their resemblance to Earthly firearms.

The new look of *Blake's 7* for its final season on the airwaves was much more raw, perhaps unromantic, stripped back and basic. Our rebels are still free of the Federation, but trapped on a dreary and dangerous planet, their future looking bleak.

What was to come was a microcosm of the previous three seasons in one, where our disparate gang of hapless heroes, trapped like prisoners on a planet without hope, would escape by chance, get a new ship, regain teleport capability, gain the speed and power to outrun Federation pursuit ships, and make efforts to hit back at the Federation.

And as with the seasons which went before, this early sense of hope and luck would eventually wear thin and the brutal oppressive might of the Federation would return with its Orwellian 'boot' to a human face.

Perhaps most importantly of all, it would be the characters that would be the driving force once again. It was Avon's unyielding attitude in 'Terminal' that led to the Liberator's doom, refusing to go around the mysterious space cloud. And it would be Avon's character that would once again prove central to the final outcome.

Behind the scenes, a number of factors would impact what ended up on the screen. The decision by actress Jan Chappell to depart the series meant the telepathic alien Cally was killed off as well.

With no alien ship, no alien handguns and no alien telepathic crew member, *Blake's 7* lost a lot of its science fiction flavour.

Suddenly it was a much more simple case of a human drama in outer space. And yet somehow this still manages to inform the final season and lend it its own, unique flavour.

And perhaps this is also appropriate because ultimately *Blake's 7* is a show about humans and their flaws and conflicts, no matter where in the universe those human conflicts might take place. Aliens and alien ships may have offered comparison or context, but it was always about the people of Earth.

Human conflict and human drama would ultimately be the central focus of the grand finale of this final season of *Blake's 7*, too. People may struggle against the forces of evil, corruption and tyranny in others, such as those in power and authority, but ultimately the struggle between good and evil takes place within us all.

Roj Blake had started out like a futuristic Robin of Sherwood, but his self-righteousness and zealotry had brought him to the brink of becoming a terrorist, a destroyer rather than a liberator of galactic civilisation.

Kerr Avon, too, had been morally grey from the start and his ascension to leadership had only seemed to escalate his paranoia, his obsessiveness and his ambiguity.

For audiences, however, season four meant one thing: *Blake's 7* were back!

It was an exciting time, a period of intense anticipation. Paul Darrow was now a big TV star, *Blake's 7* was a firmly established favourite and fans were excited to say that Avon was an amazing character, obsessive and ruthless to an almost psychotic degree, and he is the hero of the show.

It was the kind of anti-hero story that only the British would dare bring to the TV screen in 1981. While American TV was making shows with titles like *Happy Days* and *The Love Boat* and killing off regular characters was still almost unheard of in weekly TV series, *Blake's 7* was remarkably dark and fearless when it came to how it treated its 'format characters'.

The road ahead was treacherous for our heroes, leading towards a grand finale steeped in blood, gun fire and carnage!

But first, it was time to rebuild...

GAINS AND LOSSES

A lot was lost with the end of season three and the destruction of the Liberator, not to mention the departure of so many key players behind the scenes who had helped make the series what it was. Producer David Maloney was gone and so too was series creator Terry Nation.

The unexpected renewal of the series meant that David Maloney had already made other commitments and a new producer was needed. At first Terrence Dudley was considered and it is possibly a case of 'we dodged a bullet' that he turned down the job.

Dudley had been the producer of the BBC's series *Doomwatch* a few years earlier and there were allegations of Dudley alienating the creators of that series, Dr Kit Pedlar and Gerry Davis (creators of the Cybermen for *Doctor Who*) to such a degree that they quit their own show.

Dudley also produced Terry Nation's previous science fiction series *Survivors*, a show dramatizing the aftermath of a global pandemic. Allegedly, Dudley alienated Terry

Nation by taking the series in a direction which contradicted Nation's aims and intentions for the series.

Dudley would later contribute to *Doctor Who*, directing 'Meglos', a serial which under-ran and writing 'Four to Doomsday', 'Black Orchid' and 'The King's Demons'.

With Dudley not wishing to take the job, the role of producer fell to Vere Lorrimer, a man who did not have experience as a *Doctor Who* director or writer but had directed a number of *Blake's 7* episodes in previous seasons.

Possibly the most significant loss was Terry Nation departing the UK to start a new life and a new career in the United States. Although, the last minute decision of Jan Chappell to leave was also very significant.

Speaking about this decision, Chappell recalled that she felt her heart would not be in it if she were to stay and that she would not be able to give the show her all, give it the commitment it needed.

She was asked if she would consider staying for six episodes, then just for one episode or even just for a brief appearance. She finally agreed to just doing a very brief voice over for the first episode. This was, she said, her putting her foot down.

She did, however, consider that in hindsight, she perhaps should have thought of the fans and how her decision would have affected them.

Despite these reflections, at the time she decided to go, and this was a significant loss to the series.

However, Paul Darrow was now the established star of the show and he decided to stay on. The development of Avon into an increasingly obsessive, paranoid, dangerous and destructive anti-hero is the main saving grace of season four.

Yes, Paul Darrow can be over the top at times, in the series, but when the scripting is of a quality which allows for it, he really takes his character into some very interesting territory in the final season.

Some might argue that this is a departure from the cool, level headed and logical survivalist and cynic we knew from earlier seasons. But Avon had already proven he was full of surprises, such as when he abducted interrogator 'Shrinker' and shot his duplicitous lover Anna Grant.

Long-time *Blake's* 7 fan Tony Murray argues that the duff episode count is way up in season four, imparting the impression of a series some say had gone to the dogs.

However, season four has so many new elements, we could be forgiven for thinking it was almost like a new show, a kind of sequel to what went before and that the early issues were more akin to 'teething problems' before they got the bugs ironed out and the whole season was able to find its feet, as it were.

Blake's 7 fan and co-author of the fan novel 'Vindictus', Neil Shearer, suggest that Paul Darrow's acting is also poor in the final season, with some scripts depicting Avon behaving like a different character to the one he had been before, undertaking escapades that Avon, as we understood him, never would.

He also feels that Avon and Servalan, or Sleer as she calls herself, become caricatures of their original selves. Certainly there is some truth to this criticism, in terms of both the scripts and performances. Some critics even went so far as to suggest the series was less space opera and more soap opera at times, with one critic even suggesting someone needed to get Paul Darrow some acting lessons.

It would be wrong to sugar coat the truth about the final season, it definitely struggles to get on its feet with a new producer, new writers and a new ship and the results are very mixed. The restraint of the previous seasons, occasionally absent in the third season, was more apparent, with a new hand on the helm.

The VFX often feel more like a cry for help with some truly desperate measures such as the blurry orange blobs which appear in 'Stardrive' and 'Animals' as unconvincing stand-ins for the Federation pursuit ships.

In the craft of acting for the screen, sometimes very big or extreme dramatic performances are actually quite justified, such as when the sheer emotional power of a scene calls for it, but others are simply hammy and more suited to a pantomime. In the final season, there are definite lapses.

But this guide is trying to point out the things that should be appreciated and enjoyed and there is more to enjoy than there is to criticise. Subjectively speaking, it is a much better season than many of us tend to remember, and it gets very strong at times, particularly towards the end.

The second half of the season's stories are better written than the first half, possibly due to the unexpected fourth season's late announcement.

It is possible the season was rushed into production and script editor Chris Boucher may have been left scrambling to get scripts organised. Certainly there are some early stories in the season where the scripts feel as if they are raw and lacking in polish.

Long-time fans remember that there was some pre-publicity suggesting a story arc for season four in which our heroes would gather experts and advanced weapons for a final assault on the Federation.

There has been some fan speculation that

the production team had to abandon this as the collective cost of the returning guest stars would have been prohibitive.

However, it is more probable that Vere Lorrimer and Chris Boucher wanted to get the audience to believe there would be a final massive assault on the Federation, only to have it all fall apart when Avon tries to assemble allies in the penultimate episode.

This kind of deliberate wrong-footing of the audience would set the stage for the true ending, which would be far from victorious for our space rebel heroes.

One thing which is noticeable in the final season is that Robert Holmes really tries to make something of the Avon and Servalan relationship.

What had been a weird mix of attraction and mistrust in season three evolves into something considerably darker and more unnerving.

Avon's final line in 'Traitor' about Servalan is, 'I need to kill her myself' and his line in 'Orbit' about Servalan is 'she is never far from my thoughts.'

These lines of dialog are very telling and seem to suggest Robert Holmes sees Avon as harbouring a really hateful obsession with her by this point. Ironically he never gets to act on it, on screen at least.

This notion of unsatisfied hate and obsession is interesting and very different to typical depictions of television characters of the era.

Neil Shearer has argued that this obsession didn't really fit into Avon's character. However, Russell Devlin, in his response to 'Rumours of Death,' suggested Avon has an issue with betrayal due to the Anna Grant situation. Treachery and betrayal were key issues in 'The Way Back' and have been mainstays of the series as a whole. A fear of betrayal is again central to the series, notably in the last trio of episodes.

Vila feels betrayed by Avon, Zukan betrays his own daughter and our heroes, and finally, Avon believes Blake has betrayed him.

It's plausible that making Servalan pay for manipulating him and ultimately costing him the Liberator, using him like a puppet and playing him for a fool in 'Terminal,' has come to replace Avon's previous obsession with avenging Anna Grant's death.

Another key question many fans often raise about season four is why Servalan does not appear in the final episode.

There are tales of issues with Jacqueline Pearce's contract. However, an actor is contracted for a number of episodes, there is nothing dictating which episodes they must be.

Jacqueline Pearce had eight episodes in her contract, more than in any of the previous seasons. They could have made one of them the final episode of the season but chose not to, as if they did not want to. A contract is for a number of episodes, but it is not chronological.

Servalan had been introduced in the sixth episode of season one, 'Seek-Locate-Destroy' but the series had begun with faceless authority in 'The Way Back' and it is plausible the production team felt that a return to faceless authority represented by anonymous Federation troops in helmets and masks was perfect symmetry and balance, ending the show as it had begun, with pure Orwellian totalitarianism on full display.

During the fourth season, the space rebels of the Scorpio look for technological advantages (a new ship, a teleport system, a photonic star-drive propulsion system) weapons (Egrorian's Tachyon Funnel) and allies (Zukan et al), and each week there is a colourful guest star (Geoffrey Burridge, Stratford Johns, Roy Kinnear, Richard Hurndall, Stephen Yardley, etc).

But the way it ends is not with them succeeding. After a season of rising like the Phoenix from the ashes of 'Terminal' and its heart-breaking ending, it seems the rebels are now more akin to Icarus, flying closer and closer to the sun and its devastating heat, forgetting that their wings are merely composed of wax and feathers.

Their inevitable downfall is both shocking and devastating, one of the most heart-breaking and gut-wrenching hours of television drama ever broadcast in any genre.

FAREWELL TERRY NATION

One of the most significant losses to the series at the end of season three had been that of Terry Nation, who left the UK and moved along with his family to the United States, in pursuit of greater writing opportunities.

His absence from season four is acutely felt, which is interesting when we consider that many fans have often believed Chris Boucher was the true visionary behind the writing of *Blake's 7*.

There is a widely held assumption that Terry Nation had merely been in the habit of supplying the script department with little more than story outlines, which script editor Chris Boucher expanded and developed into full television scripts.

The assumption would also be that this was basically an unacknowledged writing partnership between the two men. However does it automatically follow that Terry Nation's absence would have caused a drop in quality, if Boucher was doing the lion's share of the work?

If Terry Nation's scripts were so thin, so reliant on Boucher, then why couldn't Boucher work the same magic with the work of the many new writers who came on board for season four?

Whatever the truth, Nation's engaged involvement effectively ended at 'Terminal'. Watching season four, there is a distinct feeling that something major was lost when Terry Nation departed.

There had been an assumption that *Blake's 7* would end with series C or season three as the public knew it.

Tony Murray was told the BBC announcer's voiceover confirming series four was a shock to cast and crew alike. As a result, series four was always seen as something of a postscript to the main story by many fans of the day, even while it was actually on air.

But is it true about Terry Nation only handing in story outlines, rather than rounded and completed scripts? Logically, we may doubt that any writer could get away with that and continue to be employed on *Doctor Who, The Baron, The Avengers,* the latter two as script editor or script supervisor, and being allowed to create shows like *Blake's 7* and *Survivors*.

According to Terry Nation's friend and fellow writer John Peel, Terry gave him the original scripts for his early *Doctor Who* Dalek stories and they were all quite substantial.

Yet the script editor Donald Tosh, speaking to *Doctor Who Magazine*, suggested the same notion, that Terry Nation handed in little more than story outlines on 'Dalek Master Plan'.

John Peel has intimated that the scripts Terry Nation wrote were very ambitious for the budget and therefore a lot of material was removed by the production team because it was deemed too expensive to shoot.

Other sources have suggested Terry Nation's scripts required a lot of work from script editors, too. Certainly, there is an added hint of the tone of such script editors as the funny Dennis Spooner on 'The Chase' and *Hitchhiker's Guide to the Galaxy* creator Douglas Adams on 'Destiny of the

Daleks' to suggest that Nation's scripts left room for script editors to inject something of their own.

According to Wikipedia, John Peel reinstated a lot of material that was in Terry Nation's scripts when he novelised the Dalek stories 'The Chase' and 'Dalek Master Plan', material removed due to budget constraints.

'They weren't too expensive for my budget,' John quipped.

Whatever the truth may be Terry Nation's absence from the fourth and final season of *Blake's 7* is acutely felt. It is the same show, but the whole tone and feel is quite different.

PLANNED CARNAGE OR IMPROVISED TRAGEDY?

The final season's amazing, shocking ending has many questions hanging over it. We might wonder at what point this epic ending became the decided ending for the series. If Gareth Thomas had not been willing to return as Blake one last time, or if he had simply not been available to do it, what would have been the alternative?

According to fan contributor Andrew Saunders, who was involved with *Blake's 7* fan club activities, the whole season was spent negotiating with Gareth Thomas to get him back. He was only coaxed back with the agreement and guarantee that his character would be killed off properly and permanently this time, Gareth even asked for extra blood to make his death an unmistakable fact to the viewing audience.

Years later, Gareth Thomas told interviewers that he had heard about fan theories that Blake's clone from season two episode 'Weapon' may have been the one posing as a bounty hunter on Gauda Prime and he seemed to entertain the notion that

Blake may well be alive. Like many actors who get cold feet about type casting and becoming stuck in a role, he seemed to mellow over the years to expressing some pride or fondness for the popularity his role as Roj Blake had brought him.

Fans have suggested it might have been nice to end the series with the heroes of the show somehow exposing Sleer's identity as Servalan, causing her to be arrested by the Federation and dragged off to a detention cell. This type of thing would have been a small win and some settling of the score before the big tragedy. But instead, evil or at least totalitarianism, is shown to win, going undefeated and unpunished.

So, what are the other endings which could have happened? Chris Boucher was no doubt working on the idea of the big alliance as it is dramatized in the penultimate episode, 'Warlord'. The idea that Avon would go looking for another ally after it does not work out with Zukan was a logical one.

Boucher was probably working on the final episode for some time, so the idea that they would go looking for Blake after abandoning Xenon base was probably already settled.

But if Blake could not appear, what might have happened then?

Avon certainly seems to be coming unstuck in the later part of the season, descending into a trigger happy and obsessive paranoia. This could even be construed as an onset of mental illness, possibly instigated by the stress and strain of his experiences, not the least of which include Blake going missing, Anna Grant turning out to be a fake and his own mistakes costing him the Liberator.

So Avon heading for some sort of breakdown or descent into near-madness was on the cards. What's more, his growing paranoia and obsessiveness leads them to their downfall. We might see it as a pseudo-Shakespearean descent into apparent madness, leading to ultimate tragedy.

How acceptable is this type of character development for the character? Avon was originally cold, cynical and a survivalist in the early seasons, a man of impeccable if heartless logic, more attuned to machines than people. The implication is that he is losing it, becoming unhinged or psychopathic, towards the end, possibly from a kind of mental fatigue.

How acceptable that idea is to the viewer or to the long-time fan, of course, is up to the individual. But like all things in great television drama, it is best when there is some ambiguity, some room for viewer interpretation.

Had Gareth Thomas not been able or willing to appear, perhaps the final episode would have been one of Jacqueline Pearce's appearances after all. If Gareth had pulled out, they may have had to end it with the rebel heroes arriving on Gauda Prime, believing they are coming to find Blake, only to find Blake is not there after all.

Then they could still have been ambushed for their troubles. Perhaps it could have ended with Servalan standing over Avon's bloodied corpse.

Fan Tony Murray recalls the situation on the Blake's 7 production team as the final season was nearing its final end.

He was on a set visit during the filming of

'Blake'. He and two colleagues were meant to do some work for *Blake's 7 Monthly*, the magazine which had organised the visit, but in between organising it and its happening, everyone involved with the show had been told the series was going to end, so they would all be out of work. Murray recalls, 'They weren't very welcoming to three spotty oiks up from Manchester for the day.'

It is sad to think a series as popular as *Blake's 7* was fated to be killed off, but according to producer Vere Lorrimer, if it had to end, it should end on the greatest cliff-hanger possible, hopefully one of the greatest of all time.

According to Andrew Saunders, there was a lot of rewriting of that final script. He suggests that Paul Darrow and others got involved in altering the script to get it right.

Certainly there is an interview where Paul Darrow says that when he was told Blake was to be killed off in the final episode, he said, 'I'll do it'.

A NEW DIRECTION THAT DIDN'T LAST LONG

Season three had been notably the most ensemble-based year for *Blake's 7,* offering a chance for all the regulars to get a story or three in which to really step into the spotlight and shine.

The political focus and the Blake-centric storytelling had given way to a show which allowed its supporting players to rise, expand as characters, take the spotlight and bring out the warmth, humour and drama inherent in their personalities. And the cast had taken to this with apparent enthusiasm, too.

It was also notably funnier than previous seasons, less arc-driven, more willing to play up the funny side of characters and situations, whether that meant wit or camp. It had seemed more optimistic than before, only to come back to a level of sober seriousness at the very end.

Season four would pick up from the desperately sad ending of 'Terminal', where Zen and the Liberator met their fateful end and forge a new direction for the surviving members of the rebel team.

Season four would be marked by a sense of the phoenix rising out of the ashes, too, our heroes struggling back to some level of freedom and power, but always haunted by their newfound status as the underdogs in the fight, always looking for some elusive edge on the Federation, an edge they never truly find.

Or at least, when they seem to find the ultimate means for victory, it all gets snatched away from them again.

One thing after another seems to slip through their fingers, often in the most ironic and bitter ways, and in the end, an even greater decline and fall seems to come upon them, a grim Orwellian inevitability that fate decrees they cannot avoid or overcome.

The humour and wit persists, some of the acting gets decidedly larger than life, but in the end, it is a season which sees a greater focus on real conflict and drama than ever before.

The first episode of season four, 'Rescue',

gets off to a very serious start with a bleak atmosphere and plenty of menace, but it still retains some elements from season three, as it concludes with Vila's humorous remark, 'I'm going to give up drinking, it'll be pink asteroids next!'

It had become a common practice in season three to end episodes on a light-hearted note, with episodes like 'Ultraworld' and 'Death-Watch' coming to mind as examples. But season four would soon mark out a whole new direction for the series, even if it would only last one season.

When it comes to this fourth year, there are a few standout episodes that truly encapsulate greatness. These three episodes in particular, namely 'Sand', 'Orbit', and 'Blake', can be described as nothing short of extraordinary. In fact the last five episodes see a remarkable rise in the level of drama, both from the script and acting standpoints.

Each one of these special episodes brings its own unique flair and captivating storytelling that will leave viewers on the edge of their seats.

From the imaginative visuals and Tanith

Lee's poetic writing in 'Sand' to the gripping suspense and drama in Robert Holmes' 'Orbit' to the mind-rending final twists in 'Blake', these episodes showcase the absolute pinnacle of what season four has to offer.

They demonstrate the season is capable of holding its own against the best of previous seasons.

These gems alone make season four an absolute must-watch for any fan or avid viewer seeking top-tier entertainment.

Anyone who thinks it is only since such modern series as *The Sopranos, Breaking Bad* and *Game of Thrones* that TV characters have gone to the very edge of film noir character development and human conflict may be surprised. *Blake's 7* pioneered such things in the early 1980s.

Moments such as Servalan moving the barrel of Tarrant's gun to her own head and daring him to kill her, Avon trying to hunt down his own friend to kill him out of self-preservation or breaking into hysterical laughter when his schemes go wrong, might seem strangely familiar to viewers of contemporary dramas.

But they were rare indeed when *Blake's 7* first aired. They were, to coin a phrase, ahead of their time.

And then there is the ending of the final season.

There are just no other ways to say this: *Blake's 7* will break your heart. Blake's 7 will win your heart, to be sure, but then it will break your heart. But like all great loves, the journey is well worth the heartache and the tears. Loss is awful, but as the old saying goes, it's better to have loved and lost than never to have loved at all.

But before all these things come to pass, the series must relaunch itself and 'Rescue' is a pretty great episode, for an opening episode. It is not just fun, but an absolute gem of an episode that has the power to captivate and entertain viewers with every repeated viewing.

The underlying concept of portraying *The Picture of Dorian Grey* in the realm of *Blake's 7*, was a stroke of genius by Chris Boucher.

It is reminiscent of *Doctor Who*'s penchant for crafting stories based on classic works of horror, a fact which further heightens the appreciation for 'Rescue'.

In fact, it stands among the very best episodes in season four, which unfortunately has only a limited number of such exceptional stories. Getting this one first means the season at least starts out very strong.

The first three seasons of the show were truly remarkable in their ability to create a strong sense of unity and transport viewers into a vast and awe-inspiring Universe.

The simplicity of the dramatic structure served to enhance this immersive experience, allowing viewers to truly feel like fellow travellers on a dangerous journey. One of the key elements that made these seasons so compelling was the decision to have all characters aboard the Liberator, a group of perpetual fugitives.

This dramatic choice allowed for a rich and spirited group dynamic to flourish, which undoubtedly played a significant role in the show's widespread appeal. By having everyone together in one confined space, it created an environment ripe with tension, camaraderie, and unexpected arguments, all ingredients that kept audiences eagerly coming back for more.

This not only added depth to each character's development but also provided endless opportunities for intricate storytelling. From intense conflicts to small moments of connection, every episode was infused with a palpable sense of shared adventure and fugitives-on-the-run excitement.

In essence, the decision to maintain everyone on board the Liberator throughout those initial seasons became an essential element that contributed greatly to the overall success of the show. It ensured that viewers were fully immersed in a credible situation alongside our rich and complex characters, fostering a stronger emotional connection and leaving us yearning for more.

This brings us to the situation we find here, with the Liberator gone and our heroes stranded and in disarray on Terminal.

Not only does season four dilute the essence of the story line, but it also has lost the brilliant concept of using superior alien technology in the form of a pseudo-living spaceship to combat a corrupt human administration.

This unique approach was a clever way to engage humans with something otherworldly without relying on the clichéd portrayal of poorly executed alien life forms that often plagued low budget BBC science fiction shows.

By abandoning this innovative concept, albeit unavoidably so, because the set for the Liberator was falling apart, season four lacks a key part of the appeal of *Blake's 7*.

Perhaps the Liberator set could have been replaced with some in-series explanation, but because it was decided to blow up the ship, this was not to be the case.

Somehow the Liberator's demise was appropriate for the series, destroying the ship was shocking but it was undeniably something which only *Blake's 7* would do.

Blake's 7 was distinctly different from

Doctor Who. It may look a lot like *Doctor Who*, despite eschewing time travel and alien monsters (apart from the rare exception such as the Kairos ant, which could well have escaped from *Doctor Who*'s set while no one was looking) but the major difference was that the fairy-tale optimism of *Doctor Who* was just not in the *Blake's 7* DNA.

This space adventure was more akin to a Shakespearean tragedy of epic proportions and doom tended to be final here.

The show undergoes a remarkable transformation in the fourth year, adding a fresh feel to its storylines.

Building upon the character-focused space adventure that characterized Season three, this new season aims to revive the loose arc-driven feel of the first season as the rebel heroes attempt to start over.

Notably, the sleek and elongated design of Scorpio appears to be an attempt to evoke the same enthusiasm that young viewers had for iconic spacecraft like the Millennium Falcon from *Star Wars*.

While Season four undoubtedly raises the bar with its human-centric narrative, it is important to acknowledge that some aspects may not meet everyone's expectations.

Specifically, certain sets and costumes fall short in their execution, and some of the video effects work does not fully deliver on the potential.

It is worth noting that there are some peculiar inconsistencies with the visual effects in season four.

While the model work itself is undeniably impressive, boasting some memorable new craft, the manner in which it is integrated into space backdrops using video chromakey creates a somewhat subpar appearance compared to the film shots of previous seasons.

However, these minor weaknesses in production should not overshadow the overall entertainment value of Season four and its ability to transport audiences into a universe filled with drama and adventure.

It is unfortunate that the Scorpio did not fully capitalize on its potential with a fully developed *Thunderbirds*-style launch sequence.

The underground silo and the rising launch ramp certainly suggest this idea. But while unrealised potential is always lamentable, what we do see of the Scorpio landing and taking off from Xenon base is impressive and polished.

In certain episodes, such as 'Stardrive', the visual effects seem to diminish the impact of the story instead of enhancing it. Sometimes the scripts seem to ask a little too much of the show's budget and resources.

It is noticeable that Paul Darrow's performance occasionally veers towards being overly dramatic, almost as if he is straining to salvage weak storylines single-handedly.

He starts to chew the scenery and at times he virtually devours whole sets, figuratively speaking.

However, when the scripts are on point, he does deliver some exceptional work, becoming much better as the season heads into its last half. In the end, he truly is quite brilliant, and his star power is undeniable.

And how does anyone explain the appeal of Paul Darrow and Avon? For many fans he was *Blake's 7*, the very core and essence of the series. Without him, *Blake's 7* would have been a much poorer experience.

Describing him is a challenge for any fan.

His face resembled the famous marble busts of ancient Roman Emperors and Generals, handed down to our civilisation from antiquity. His prominent nose, large eyes and distinct cupid's bow top lip give him a face that seems well suited to playing a legendary or iconic figure.

Darrow himself seems to have been well aware of his character's potential. He once stated he saw Avon as possibly the best character on the show. He sets out to prove it, too.

In his acting style, he moves slowly and deliberately, like a panther stalking about its turf, relaxed, unhurried but always watching. He underacts, overacts, but rarely just acts, always taking Avon to the most interesting destination, rather than the most obvious.

By the time season four or series D was airing, it seemed fans could not discuss the series without their sisters or mothers interrupting their discussions to mention how much they liked the handsome Avon.

By this point in the show, his season three make-over had developed to include a black costume with metal studs, blow-waved hair in a style similar to the early George Michael and even gloves and boots.

In personality, Avon was cold and calculating, yet could smile easily, as well. His one-liners and zingers were a mix of *Blackadder* sarcasm and *James Bond* black humour.

But he was not just caustic; his sarcasm was intellectual, his criticisms expressed with skill and grace.

And his character arc was fascinating to watch, as he grew or descended into a trigger happy, paranoid, volatile, explosive antihero who could laugh into the abyss and grin into the face of death itself.

Avon was a fascinating, intriguing character, all in all. He was a rather dangerous and unpredictable man, ruthless and possibly a sociopath, if not an actual psychopath.

And he was on our side.

BLAKE'S 7 FOURTH SEASON THOUGHTS

RUSSELL DEVLIN

For a series as popular as it was and with such a devoted following, *Blake's 7* had a very precarious life. Pulled out of the hat as a last minute pitch to the BBC by Terry Nation and almost improvised into the first season, it was never quite sure if it would be renewed, hence the cliff-hanger endings to each series.

While the fourth season continued to be a ratings winner, it was communicated from on high at the BBC that they did really want to finish it off this time and so the production team were determined to do so in a shock ending, one which is still talked about till this day.

Apparently the decision for a fourth series was made literally at the last minute of the third. Allegedly the BBC controller liked season three closer 'Terminal' so much that he green lit another series and it was announced over the closing credits, much to the surprise of the production staff, who had just destroyed the set and the miniature of the Liberator, thinking they wouldn't need them anymore.

They quickly got things in motion again but found that Jan Chappell didn't want to come back, as she had been disappointed in the way her character had been developed (which is why Sally Knyvette had left after season 2) and also wanted to be a full time mother to her new child.

She was unwilling to shoot a departure scene, so she had a very unsatisfactory (from the audience's perspective) off-camera death as the crew attempted to escape Servalan's Terminal complex.

Jacqueline Pearce was also not thought to be available, as she suffered from bouts of severe clinical depression (which was not generally known to the shows fans at the time) so the replacement character 'Sleer' was developed, but Jacquie recovered enough to re-join the cast.

Sleer was used as her alias with the backstory that Servalan had been toppled in a coup while she was busy on Terminal (a plotline used in season three's 'Rumours of Death) and was secretly trying to regain power.

This led to some dubious plot points and timing issues in subsequent stories, as in short order she escaped Terminal, became Sleer, set up a highly successful planetary pacification programme and murdered a large number of Federation officials who recognised her, but *Blake's 7* was no stranger to those.

New character Soolin, Dorian's gunslinger partner, pragmatically joins up with the seven when he tries to throw them all to an old Sea Devil, or at least a man in one of their costumes, is a character cast in the same mould of Dayna and Tarrant.

Young and attractive with a very violent backstory and hard-nosed attitude, she was portrayed by the glamorous Glynis Barber and reinforced the show's trend away from the original band of political rebels to space freebooters who fight for survival rather than a political ideal.

While Glynis is a distinguished actor, Soolin was the least well characterised member of the *Blake's 7* team and never evolved beyond the initial ruthless and sexy gunslinger description, and never received her own Soolin-centric episode, unlike the show's other characters.

A new spaceship was required and arrived in the form of the Scorpio, designed by Jim Francis and built by Rob Thornton, much to Martin Bower's chagrin.

Scorpio was an elderly 100 metre or so planet hopper used by the mysterious Dorian to get around in, and unlike the giant alien Liberator was much more akin to what was being seen in *Star Wars, Buck Rogers* and the like.

Though augmented by Dr Plaxton's stardive in episode four, the ship was no match for its Federation opponents and does not even get to fire its guns at them.

Interestingly in the *'Blake's 7 Monthly'* comic strip adaption, it becomes more of a mini-Liberator, reflecting the demands of that type of storytelling.

The interior set ate up the budget and while effective for what it is, it lacked the scope and effectiveness of the Liberator set. A new title sequence was also required and while again it is effective enough, many bemoaned its absence of spaceships or cast.

Jim Francis and Steve Drewett's FX team did a good set of establishing shots of the Scorpio and sequences of it entering and leaving its planet Xenon base that were worthy of a Gerry and Sylvia Anderson production.

Unfortunately, in a similar situation to Ian Scoones' series one London spaceship shots, they blew the FX budget on these, so the rest of the seasons space shots were done using quicker and easier chromakey video effects.

Of course, the use of chromakey and video tape meant these were far inferior to the filmed shots, a situation made worse by their abundance.

The episode 'Stardrive' for example contains as many FX shots as a feature film with some of great complexity, but the end result was often risible and this brings the story down, particularly in scenes such as when Federation Pursuit ships are reduced to wobbly red blobs in an otherwise dramatically tense closing scene.

There was also a new Producer, as David Maloney had moved on to the gritty drama series 'When the Boat Comes in' and was replaced by Vere Lorrimer . Maloney had been part of Phillip Hinchcliffe's Tom Baker *Doctor Who* team which had taken an adult and frequently violent approach to the series (ie 'Genesis of the Daleks', 'Talons of Weng Chiang') and Maloney had very much carried this over to *Blake's 7*.

Vere was a veteran TV producer and director having worked in the industry since the 1950's, and was no stranger to *Blake's 7*, having directed a dozen episodes, but there is a different feel to his stories. The format change from the Federation trying to capture the Liberator and Blake or Avon to the seven trying to gather weapons and allies or trying to disrupt the Federation plans had an overall nihilistic theme, with the resurgent power of the Federation hanging over the show like a pall of smoke.

The pressures of setbacks, betrayals and leadership make Avon progressively paranoid and survivalist, even Dudley Simpson's incidental music reflects this, the heroic and optimistic themes of the earlier series are largely replaced by the dark strains of the Federation.

Curiously this dark approach was balanced by a not infrequent campiness. Sometimes this was due to budget limitations or the flights of fancy of costume designers, but in 'Assassin' it was very deliberate, with the over the top and halfway to Berlin performances of Betty Marsden as the Slave Trader and Caroline Holdaway as simpering Piri and utterly nuts Cancer.

John Savident as the lovesick Egrorian was another scenery chewer in a performance which is a huge contrast to his earlier *Blake's 7* role in 'Trial', but this worked as a counterpoint to the harrowing attempt of Avon to sacrifice Vila to save himself.

The ultimate 'Have you betrayed us, have you, betrayed me?' denouement is almost inevitable, though Vere did not want to give the game away, in interviews in the fan media he said that the series would see the *Blake's 7* crew gathering and assembling a series of inventions and weapons together, leading to an ultimate attack on Earth, which is a feasible format or story arc up to and including 'Warlord'.

They did however want to go out in a way that would be remembered, though still left a possible line open to another series or even a revival.

Attempts were made in this regard and indeed there has been a quite a number of BBC and Big Finish Audio adventures and even a reboot radio series, but with an ending which is hard to top, perhaps it is best just to leave them with the blaring sirens of Gauda Prime.

RESCUE

Cally is dead - a victim of Servalan's booby trapped bequest of a planet. The Liberator has been destroyed. With Avon colder than ever, the crew must raise the will to fight on for their lives. Cue the enigmatic Dorian with an escape route off Terminal and the offer of friendship. (Plot description from the VHS release summary)

The destruction of the Liberator leaves the crew marooned on the enigmatic planet Terminal.

Their sole chance of escape is through Servalan's rigged ship, which unfortunately leads to Cally's death in a subsequent explosion. This blast also annihilates the subterranean base and sets off a series of chain reactions across the whole planet.

In no time, a vessel named Scorpio makes its appearance, steered by a salvage worker known as Dorian. The planet is on the brink of annihilation, so Avon and Tarrant resort to threatening Dorian, to force him into helping them escape.

Succumbing to their pressure, Dorian transports them to his intricate subterranean headquarters on planet Xenon where they encounter his associate, Soolin.

Upon establishing his presence, Dorian cunningly disarms the team's weapons and unveils his ambitious plans. He intends to leverage Orac's capabilities to construct a functional teleport system for his vessel.

However, a sinister secret shadows him: an unending bond with a life-sapping creature that dwells in the caverns beneath his stronghold. His chilling intent is to offer up the Liberator crew as sacrificial lambs to this entity. They will in effect become part of it.

The first episode of Series D, the fourth and final season of *Blake's 7* experienced some last-minute changes behind the scenes due to its eleventh-hour renewal.

Jan Chappell, who chose not to return as Cally, provided a voiceover for Cally's off-screen demise. Moreover, David Maloney, the show's producer since the beginning, had moved on, and Vere Lorrimer took over his role. The initial script for Series D was written with the expectation that all cast members, including Cally, would reprise their roles.

In an unprecedented move, Terry Nation did not write the script for the season premiere. His initial plan was to conclude the series with the third season finale. But when the BBC opted for a fourth season, Nation decided to step back.

In September 1980, he and his wife Kate left Britain for Los Angeles where he kept busy planning and developing new projects for various studios like Columbia, 20th Century Fox, and MGM.

Despite his efforts though, success in the US remained elusive and *Blakes 7* ended up being his final notable contribution to television history.

He did, however, work on *McGyver* and the *Doctor Who* TV movie which featured Paul McGann, where he revived Dalek planet Skaro, last seen blown up at the end of TV serial 'Remembrance of the Daleks', true to his motto, 'never kill anything off'.

In this episode, the character Slave is voiced by Peter Tuddenham. However, he is only credited as Orac in all episodes of the fourth season, except for '*Blake*'.

It's interesting to note that the creature's costume is actually a repurposed Sea Devil outfit from *Doctor Who*.

The original script for this episode had several scenes and dialogue that didn't make it to the final broadcast. One example is the extended interaction between Dorian and Slave. In this version, Dorian asks Slave to investigate the cause of Liberator's explosion and hints at his plans for the crew, which go beyond a simple rescue mission.

The character Dorian was inspired by the main character in Oscar Wilde's novel, *The Picture of Dorian Gray*. This narrative revolves around an innocent young man who spirals into moral decay after acquiring immortality.

In the Oscar Wilde story, a portrait of Dorian as a youthful individual is created.

Interestingly, this portrait absorbs all of Dorian's transgressions and physical signs of aging.

For 18 years, Dorian indulges in a life filled with hedonism. In the end, his life concludes tragically as he attempts to free himself from the curse imposed by his own painting.

Chris Boucher's adaptation uses the basic themes, with an added dose of science fantasy and a repurposed Sea Devil. The results are suitably horrific, although Geoff Burridge's screaming and wailing death scenes are perilously close to laugh-inducing in their intensity.

This Dorian has lived 200 years, thanks to a subterranean chamber which somehow allows his corruption to be absorbed by a man who has been trapped down there.

His plot to replace this victim with Avon and his friends gives Chris Boucher the opportunity to emphasise the bond which exists between the rebels, a nice reminder of the way our heroes have become a unit.

Michael Keating is superb as usual as Vila,

getting one of his finest moments when he appears behind Dorian with a gun in his hand, only to hear Dorian explain to Avon that all the guns have been rendered useless. Vila looks at the gun, realises it will be useless too and rolls his eyes. It's a perfectly pitched moment of silent comedy.

In the end, it is Vila who hands Avon a Federation gun, the only gun that still works, allowing Avon a chance to shoot the creature and bring the horror of Dorian to a grisly end, aging to death and turning to dust. Any story where Vila saves the day is a good one and our heroes are now well and truly back in business.

RESCUE

REVIEWED BY
KEN DEEP

Series D opens with the aptly titled episode 'Rescue'. Presumably it implies safety. It could also have been called 'Return'. Our crew are mostly back. The show has returned, but more accurately it was also 'Rescued' from an early end. In late March 1980 the cast and crew of Blake's 7 believed 'Terminal' was the end of their journey.

A surprise voiceover told the world that the BBC had other plans. A fourth series was commissioned. Lore tells of a BBC controller whose wife was a fan of the show influencing her husband, but the truth may be more practical. An additional set of episodes creates a lucrative syndication package.

The show was given a moment to reset. There's a change of tone in series D, a chance to reinvent challenges for our crew. A new ship, a new computer, even a new base from which to strike at the remains of the totalitarian Federation, are all introduced.

There was also a chance to add new series regulars. The beautiful gunslinger Soolin became 'Han Solo for the dads'. But there was a missed opportunity to introduce a character into the mixture who would continue the show's tradition of subverting expectations.

The guest character of Dorian, a thinly veiled retelling of Oscar Wilde's *The Picture of Dorian Grey*, would have given the remaining characters someone whose motives are as opaque as theirs.

Like a vampire, Dorian would have needs that are morally ambiguous. His requirements would include feeding on other human beings. And we might ponder the way this reflects the early episodes of the first season where the Mutoids were nicknamed vampires for the way they needed to consume 'blood serum' to survive.

Dorian is a formidable character, too. His intellect rivals Avon's. His piloting and weapons expertise would challenge Tarrant and Dayna. Even his girlfriend Soolin would not be off limits, if his needs depended.

It's disappointing that he was dispatched

like so many other villains of the week.

The tools the crew were given in the first series were exciting. They had the mightiest spaceship, teleport capability, and two incredible computers.

Now, in the fourth and final series, our team are ragtag. Enter Dorian, with all of his genius, into the group and there would be the feeling of being ahead of their adversaries.

The Federation was on its heels after Star One. If only this crew had an advantage.

An advantage needed to deliver the final act...

THE SLAVE COMPUTER'S MOST HUMBLE ASSESSMENT OF THE SITUATION:

9/10

A NEW SHIP:

FROM LIBERATOR TO SCORPIO

In the sci-fi universe of *Blake's 7*, the ships are more than just vessels; they're characters in their own right, each with its own personality and significance to the story.

One of the most notable transitions in the series occurs when the iconic ship, the Liberator, is replaced by a new craft named Scorpio. This shift marks a significant moment in the narrative and introduces a host of new dynamics for the crew and viewers alike.

First there is the question of origins and ownership.

The Liberator, a marvel of alien technology, was a mysterious and powerful presence throughout the early seasons of *Blake's 7*. Its acquisition by the crew was a stroke of fate, thrusting them into a world of rebellion and resistance.

However, when the Liberator met its demise, a new era dawned with the introduction of Scorpio. Unlike its predecessor, Scorpio is a human-built ship, reflecting a shift from reliance on external, enigmatic, alien forces to the more familiar creations of human engineering and ingenuity. One might call this a little more mundane and ordinary.

The technology and design are very different, too. While both ships are advanced spacecraft, they differ significantly in their design and technology. The Liberator, with its angular and iconic appearance, exuded an air of otherworldly sophistication.

In contrast, Scorpio is smaller, more basic and more workmanlike in design. This change in aesthetics symbolizes a departure from the empowering and exciting fantasy of the show's past and sets the stage for new, gritty, functional space adventures.

The role of the ship's computer changes, as well. One of the most notable differences between the Liberator and Scorpio is their on-board computer systems. The Liberator was equipped with Zen, a wise and autonomous entity that served as a trusted advisor to the crew.

The deep sense of sorrow that enveloped viewers when Zen seemingly 'died' in Terminal truly highlighted Peter Tuddenham's exceptional talent as a voice actor and underscored the remarkable ability of the writing to evoke genuine emotions towards a mere machine - a dome with flickering lights, almost making us feel as though it possessed human-like qualities.

Viewers strongly link Zen with the Liberator, emphasizing its significance within the narrative. Zen served as the heart and soul of the ship, embodying a crucial role in the dynamics of the crew's interactions and operations.

When he died, he said, 'I have failed you!' Zen and the Liberator were two aspects of an almost human craft. The loss was powerful and distressing to see.

In contrast, Scorpio features a humble and subservient computer named Slave.

This shift in dynamic, from lofty autonomy to comical, grovelling subservience, impacts how the crew interacts with the ship, how they make decisions, altering their relationship with technology and furthering the sense that they are now underdogs, more than ever before.

Cultural influences and an effort to increase audience appeal are also apparent in this beginning to the final season.

The transition from the Liberator to Scorpio occurred during the peak of *Star Wars* popularity, leading some to speculate whether the design of Scorpio was influenced by the iconic Millennium Falcon.

While similarities between the two ships are apparent, it's important to recognize that sci-fi aesthetics often draw from broader trends in the genre, too. Whether intentional or coincidental, the resemblance may have served to attract viewers familiar with *Star Wars* while also establishing Scorpio as a distinct entity, within *Blake's 7's* fictional universe.

In conclusion, this bold new direction for the series is a significant change from Terry Nation's original vision.

The shift from the Liberator to Scorpio

represents more than just a change in spacecraft; it's a narrative turning point that introduces new dynamics and possibilities for the crew and viewers alike.

From the origins of the ships to their design and technology, each aspect contributes to the rich atmosphere of the series and invites audiences to embark on a new chapter in the ongoing saga of rebellion and adventure in the far reaches of space.

The transition to Scorpio is a pivotal moment in the series, marked by changes in origin, technology, and narrative dynamics. As viewers journey alongside the crew aboard the new ship, they are reminded that in the vast expanse of space, every vessel tells a story of its own.

POWER

With Avon in the hands of primitive warriors and the silo door to Scorpio impossible to open without him, things look bleak food-wise for the survivors of the Liberator. Then Vila discovers Dorian's nuclear compression charge and suddenly the future of the whole base is at stake. (VHS release summary)

Dorian's demise and Soolin's disappearance have left the remaining crew members stranded in an underground base. Their only escape route, the freighter Scorpio, is blocked by a security door that even Vila can't crack open.

The situation escalates when Vila stumbles upon a 'nuclear compression bomb' set up by Dorian with a ticking countdown timer. If it detonates, it will generate a temporary black hole large enough to obliterate the entire base.

On the planet's surface, Avon finds himself in a tight spot, captured by the Hommicks. This native male tribe is embroiled in a bitter gender conflict with the Seska - a dwindling female tribe with telekinetic abilities amplified by an uncommon dynamon crystal.

In the end, the remaining two Seskas manage to disarm the bomb. However, when the door opens, one of them named Pella attempts to seize control of Scorpio, killing her companion in the process.

Avon, with Orac's assistance, uses the deceased Seska's crystal to finalize Dorian's teleporter and successfully eliminates Pella - the last standing Seska. Following these events, Soolin emerges from her hiding spot and decides to become a part of Avon's team.

REBUILDING POWER:

THEMES OF ADAPTATION AND AMBITION

'Power' opens with a compelling narrative situation, introducing a world torn apart by a gender-based conflict on the planet Xenon. This conflict, fuelled by the acquisition and use of powerful crystals known as dynamon, sets the stage for a dramatization of power dynamics. Some might argue it does not fully deliver on its promise, but there are moments that provoke thought.

With the destruction of the Liberator, which had the advantage of teleportation capability, Avon sees an opportunity to rebuild and regain control by harnessing the power of the dynamon crystals for a new purpose: to power a teleport system for the newly acquired ship, Scorpio.

The symbolism embedded in Avon's quest is multifaceted. On one level, it represents the heroes' determination to adapt and overcome the setbacks they faced in previous seasons.

The loss of the Liberator could have been a crushing blow, but instead, it becomes a catalyst for innovation and reinvention. Avon's vision for the Scorpio reflects a broader theme of resilience in the face of adversity, a testament to the characters' ability to adapt to changing circumstances and forge ahead, in the pursuit of their goals.

Moreover, Avon's ambition to harness the power of the dynamon crystals for teleportation technology speaks to larger themes of resourcefulness and ingenuity.

In a world where power is often synonymous with physical strength or technological superiority, the episode presents the notion of women who have harnessed their strength and can direct it as telekinesis against men.

However, Avon's quest for power is not without its moral complexities. The conflict on Xenon, fuelled by the use of dynamon crystals as weapons, serves as a cautionary tale about the dangers of unchecked ambition and the destructive consequences of power struggles.

In essence, *Blake's 7* offers us a compelling exploration of power, ambition, and resilience in Avon's quest to rebuild and reassert control in the wake of the Liberator's destruction.

The power struggle in the battle of the sexes which has raged on the surface of Xenon is provocative, too. Gun-Sarr is an amusing yet unnerving brute and although Avon is typically powerful and dominant in the episode's finale, it is hard not to feel sorry for the ambitious final member of the Seska when Avon kills her.

It is worth mentioning that this is the only episode in which anyone refers to Dayna's skin colour. One of the Seska women, watching her in a fight against Gunn-Sar, says, 'the black woman must win.'

Dayna appears in 26 episodes of *Blake's 7* and this is the only time she is referred to this way. The rest of the time she is simply referred to as Dayna, a human woman of Earth ancestry, one of *Blake's 7*, a rebel.

We are always invited to view her by the content of her character, the same as the others, never by the colour of her skin.

The scenes of combat with Gun-Sarr position this episode in the same vein as 'Duel', 'Harvest of Kairos' and 'Death Watch' and cements the duel to the death between two opponents as one of the standard tropes of *Blake's 7*.

Vila's ramblings about the compression charge and his concern that he may have 'brain warp' are a nice amusing touch.

SOOLIN

In addition to the challenges of rebuilding their power and navigating the ethical complexities of their actions, the crew of *Blake's 7* also faces the loss of a key member, Cally.

As an alien with telepathic abilities hailing from the enigmatic planet Auron, Cally brought a sense of mystery and depth to the series, embodying the complexities of the universe in which the characters operate.

Cally's departure leaves a void within the crew, both in terms of her unique abilities and her rich backstory. Her telepathic powers added an intriguing dimension to the dynamics on-board the Liberator, providing insights and perspectives that were often crucial to the success of their missions.

Furthermore, her origins on Auron hinted at a larger universe filled with untold stories and unexplored mysteries, contributing to the sense of wonder and possibility that permeated the series.

In her place, a new character is introduced—a capable individual with proficiency in combat but lacking the otherworldly qualities and depth of Cally.

While new addition Soolin brings her own skills and strengths to the table, her presence underscores the challenge of replacing a character as multifaceted and compelling as Cally.

Without the mystery of Cally's alien origins and telepathic abilities, the crew must navigate their new dynamic and find new ways to adapt and succeed in their missions.

The introduction of this new character reflects the broader theme of rebuilding and finding new directions.

Just as Avon seeks to repurpose resources and innovate in the wake of the Liberator's destruction, the crew must also adapt to changes within their ranks.

While the loss of Cally may be felt deeply by both the characters and the audience, it also presents an opportunity for growth and exploration as the series continues to evolve.

In this sense, the departure of Cally and the introduction of a new character serve as yet another chapter in the ongoing saga *of Blake's 7*—a saga defined by its ability to adapt, reinvent, and find new avenues for storytelling even in the face of adversity.

Sadly, Soolin is not really given much backstory aside from the opening episode and the very last one, both written by Chris Boucher.

And there is no on-screen attempt to explain or justify why she would have an issue with Servalan. Perhaps ultimately it can be seen as a case of 'the enemy of my friends is my enemy too'.

The charismatic and talented Glynis Barber manages to make the character both admirable and likeable, with a solid acting performance. Her striking blonde hair and confident manner are immediately a hit with the audience.

THE SLAVE COMPUTER'S MOST HUMBLE ASSESSMENT OF THE SITUATION:

8/10

TRAITOR

The Federation is rebuilding its empire at a breakneck speed and the planet Helotrix is its latest conquest. Avon and the crew are intrigued. How could the tenacious Helots have caved in so quickly? Just what is the Federation's new weapon? What has happened to Servalan? (VHS release summary)

The Federation is growing at a concerning pace, and with the recent inclusion of Helotrix, Avon feels compelled to investigate their methods. He dispatches Dayna and Tarrant for reconnaissance.

Soon enough, they encounter a resistance faction headed by a man called Hunda.

The Federation's use of a fast-acting pacification drug, Pylene-50, comes to light. The operation is spearheaded by a fresh security commissioner named Sleer.

Assisted by Hunda, Tarrant and Dayna manage to connect with Leitz - a Federation officer who has been secretly feeding information to the resistance.

Leitz discloses the production location of the drug and hints at a potential antidote. Ignoring Avon's directive to stay out of it, Tarrant resolves to halt this operation.

Contrary to initial beliefs, Leitz isn't a traitor. He's actually working under Sleer's directives to orchestrate an ambush.

When the trap is finally triggered, Tarrant and Dayna get their first look at the elusive Commissioner Sleer – who shockingly turns out to be Servalan.

This story is perhaps a little dull and static at times, yet there's no denying Robert Holmes does something very interesting by introducing us to a sort of spoiled, indulgent and decoratively uniformed officer class of the Federation who like to live it up like the Nazi High Command.

Stylish sets and costumes are presented for these sequences too. Holmes' first few *Blake's 7* scripts really feel like they have too much going on in them, as if he was still thinking in terms of a 90 minute, four-part format like he used on *Doctor Who*.

The ending of the episode is worth the wait

and makes it clear that Servalan is back in business. The script seems to be written with a solid grasp of *Blake's 7*'s strengths in production terms, too, because the whole thing looks remarkably high in production values.

The way Servalan allows Leitz to think he can use her as his plaything only to eliminate him like a black widow is a classic moment for her character.

With his eye patch and his apparent designs on Servalan, viewers could be forgiven for thinking that Leitz is being introduced as a latter day equivalent to Travis, only to see him killed as Servalan turns the tables on him.

Particularly notable is Avon's reaction to the news that Servalan escaped the destruction of the Liberator. He says he did not want her to die that way, which at first sounds as if he might be expressing some form of compassion for her.

But this is a classic case of Robert Holmes wrong-footing the audience. His next line, which ends the episode, is the stunning, 'I need to kill her myself.'

It's the beginning of the potent direction in which Avon's character will evolve in the final season, becoming increasingly dark, obsessive, paranoiac and unpredictable.

While Paul Darrow could be said to be too Shakespearean and too theatrical, sometimes staring obsessively into the middle distance as if giving a stage performance, there seems to be a thought behind it all, a descent into a very dark place, almost as if the intention is for something akin to 'Hamlet' or 'Macbeth'.

Despite the ups and downs of the production around him, Avon is the main reason to keep watching.

DING DONG, THE WITCH IS ALIVE

The enigmatic and formidable presence of Servalan, the cunning antagonist and iconic villainess of *Blake's 7*, left audiences in suspense at the end of season three.

With her unexpected acquisition of the Liberator just moments before its explosive demise, fans were left pondering her fate. Was she alive or dead? The tantalizing ambiguity surrounding her character fuelled speculation and anticipation for her eventual return.

In the eagerly awaited return story 'Traitor,' Servalan emerges from the shadows once more, alive but with a twist.

Concealing her true identity under the guise of Commissioner Sleer, she navigates the intricate webs of power and deception with her trademark cunning and manipulation. The galaxy thinks Servalan is dead and she wants to keep it that way, for her own ends.

Producer Vere Lorrimer told Starburst magazine in the lead up to the season's television debut that the name Sleer was derived from a combination of two words: sly and sneer.

The revelation of her survival is welcome to fans, reigniting the tension between our protagonists and their number one adversary once again. She would go on to appear in a total of eight episodes of the season, cementing her place as the face of the enemy in *Blake's 7*.

Servalan's ability to adapt and thrive in the face of adversity showcases her indomitable cunning and insatiable thirst for power.

Like the best film noir characters, she is both monstrous and, somehow, a character we love and even feel some empathy for.

As she manoeuvres through the shadows, her presence looms large, casting a palpable sense of intrigue and apprehension over the storyline.

For fans of *Blake's 7*, the return of Servalan is a highlight. Her reappearance injects a renewed excitement and uncertainty into the narrative. The wicked witch is alive, and her spellbinding presence continues to captivate and enthral us.

THE

SLAVE COMPUTER'S

MOST HUMBLE

ASSESSMENT OF THE

SITUATION:

8/10

STARDRIVE

With her main drive unit damaged beyond repair, the Scorpio and the crew will be stranded on the base unless they can find a replacement. Dr. Plaxton and her drive prototype provide a dream solution, except there's one problem - she's working for the Space Rats. (VHS release summary)

The team attempts to covertly infiltrate a system swarming with patrols in their quest for fuel. Aware of Scorpio's sluggish speed, Avon opts for a daring strategy: to glide undetected by hugging an asteroid.

However, this risky move backfires as they end up crashing into it instead.

During the repair work, the team shockingly observes three Federation ships mysteriously blowing up.

Upon further investigation of these explosions, they find out that these ships were ambushed by extremely swift spacecraft.

These unidentified vessels are recognized as space choppers by Orac, which interestingly use an experimental photon drive. This advanced technology is the brainchild of a non-conformist scientist known as Dr Plaxton.

Avon has made the decision to employ this drive for Scorpio. However, obtaining one requires them to locate Plaxton, who is currently under the employment of the Space Rats. This group is essentially a bunch of unhinged misfits living on planet Caspar.

In a typical *Blake's 7* twist, the Space Rats have a leader who is not a Space Rat at all, but a cunning and greedy mastermind who plans to use the criminal gang for his own ends, hoping to become a powerful force in the galaxy.

Avon, ever the intriguing and pragmatic anti-hero, uses Vila and Dayna as part of his own strategy to get the star-drive for Scorpio and when things go wrong, he sacrifices Dr Plaxton with the icy cold efficiency and utter ruthlessness of a machine.

GETTING UP TO SPEED.

It is such a shame 'Stardrive' is let down in production somewhat, at least in terms of visual effects and costuming because there is a lot to like about it.

The opening where Avon all but wrecks the ship and Vila plays him to get him to fix it using his ideas is really great.

The whole episode begins with plenty of tension and Michael Keating steals the show with a terrific comic performance.

There's some great dialog too, such as when they realise they have air for several days, leading Soolin to comment that when it finally runs out, 'we'll be bored, as well as dead.'

The ending of the episode where Dr Plaxton is sacrificed by Avon to the God of icy cold logic is also superb, reminding us of what a breath-takingly ruthless anti-hero he really is.

If the Space Rats rather silly and over the top outfits, and the appalling orange blobs standing in for pursuit ships, were not there to undermine it, this episode could become a favourite.

Certainly the human aspect of the episode has real power.

'NAVIGATING MORAL AMBIGUITY:

AVON'S CALCULATED SACRIFICE IN THE DEPTHS OF SPACE'

The saga of the Scorpio stands as a testament to the relentless pursuit of survival amidst the vast expanse of the cosmos. Or does it? Once propelled by the nimble prowess of the Liberator, the crew now finds themselves grappling with the aged and sluggish confines of their current vessel. A scruffy bucket of bolts!

The Space Rats, a notorious band of interstellar miscreants, pose a formidable threat to the Scorpio and its crew. In a bid to reclaim their edge, they embark on a perilous mission to secure a crucial engine upgrade from scientist, Dr Plaxton.

However, as fate would have it, the pursuit of technological advancement becomes entwined with moral quandaries of the gravest nature. Avon, renowned for his unwavering logic and unwavering pragmatism, faces a harrowing dilemma.

In a moment that reverberates with the weight of cosmic consequence, he makes the fateful decision to sacrifice the life of Dr. Plaxton.

Avon's rationale is as chilling as the void of space itself: the survival of the crew hinges upon the sacrifice of one. In a cold calculus of self-preservation, he deems Dr. Plaxton expendable, rationalizing that her demise ensures the continued existence of the collective.

This sombre juncture forces us to confront the moral complexities inherent in the pursuit of survival. Avon's choice, though steeped in pragmatism, serves as a stark reminder of the moral tightrope.

As we reflect upon the trials of the Scorpio and its crew, it is the choices made in the face of adversity that define the very essence of humanity.

Nonetheless, it's hard not to be stunned when Avon is asked about Dr Plaxton at the end of the episode and he simply responds, 'Who?'

THE SLAVE COMPUTER'S MOST HUMBLE ASSESSMENT OF THE SITUATION:

7/10

ANIMALS

Intent on recruiting experts in the fight against the Federation's pacification programme, Tarrant and Dayna set a course for Bucol 2 and Dayna's old lover and mentor Justin, renowned genetic engineer. Then the Scorpio comes under attack and Tarrant has to pull out, leaving Dayna down on the planet with Servalan on her way. (VHS release summary)

Dayna and Tarrant land on the planet Bucol II, with Dayna on a mission to find Justin, her father's old associate who happens to be a genetic scientist. Upon arrival, she encounters bizarre humanoid creatures that attack her. Luckily, Justin comes to her rescue just in time.

In space, Scorpio faces an onslaught from Federation ships, compelling Tarrant to leave Dayna behind and retreat for necessary repairs.

Meanwhile on Bucol, Dayna attempts to

persuade Justin to assist in creating a cure for the Federation's tranquillizing drug.

However, she is horrified by his past involvement in developing genetically enhanced super-soldiers for the Federation - a fact underscored by the monstrous creatures he engineered.

In the meantime, Servalan gets wind of Justin's clandestine project on Bucol and decides to probe further. She successfully ensnares Dayna and manipulates her mind to assist in trapping her own friend.

But this is a complicated situation. Servalan deduces that Dayna loves Justin. Using a form of aversion therapy, she transforms Dayna's love for Justin into hate.

Later, Servalan reverses the processing, allowing Dayna's love for Justin to be restored in time for her to mourn his death.

We might look at this episode and conclude that we should never underestimate what kind of man a woman finds attractive. That is practically a life lesson for men.

However, the character of Justin is a bit of a stretch for most viewers to accept, particularly considering their backstory includes a role as student and mentor. Dayna's guns are mentioned as something Justin was aware of. Assuming she was not developing fire arms as a child, we may take this to mean Dayna was a young woman at the time she met Justin, but nevertheless, it is a backstory which alienates viewers.

Dayna crying over him is not going to be high on many people's lists of touching moments. What's more, the plot involving Servalan conditioning Dayna to hate the man she loves, and reversing it, takes place in the last 15 minutes of the episode. It feels rushed and forced and lacks credibility. Something more subtle might have been a better idea for the storyteller.

Another issue with the episode is that the most popular characters, Avon, Vila and Orac, along with Soolin and Tarrant, get very little screen time until the finale.

There's a hilarious scene with Avon pressuring the hapless Vila to submerge himself in a smelly, horrible ballast tank underneath the Scorpio which involves Vila demanding a glass of wine as a reward and Avon responding 'half a glass'. But while this is fun, it's all too brief.

There is also a nice guest appearance from science fiction stalwart Kevin Stoney, his character dying at the hands of Servalan. But again, it's a small positive.

A great deal of screen time goes to Dayna and Justin. They are not particularly sympathetic or involving together. One theory is that the story was planned for Cally and was hastily rejigged for Dayna when Jan Chappell decided to quit the series.

Whatever the behind the scenes situation, the episode never really takes off and much of the dialog is heavy handed and lacking the usual crisp, witty or elegant style *Blake's 7* is known and respected for.

However, the basic ideas which underpin the episode are sound enough and in some respects, quite strong. And this is typical of *Blake's 7*.

ETHICAL DILEMMAS

WHO ARE THE REAL ANIMALS?

In the vast expanse of science fiction television, certain episodes stand out not just for their entertainment value, but for their exploration of ethical quandaries. 'Animals' should be one of these episodes, at least if we consider the premise and the ideas which underpin the script.

Scientific Experimentation on Animals is always a touchy topic. In 'Animals', viewers are introduced to scientist Justin, whose work leads him to conduct experiments aimed at creating intelligent animal servants.

This premise immediately draws parallels to H.G. Wells' classic novel, *The Island of Dr. Moreau*, wherein the titular character engages in grotesque experiments to uplift animals to human-like intelligence.

The portrayal of Justin's experiments forces viewers to grapple with the moral implications of testing on animals for the advancement of science and potential military applications.

The ethical questions raised by Justin's experiments are multifaceted. On one hand, there's the utilitarian argument that such experiments could lead to significant scientific breakthroughs, potentially benefiting humanity as a whole.

However, this perspective often overlooks the suffering endured by the animals involved, something which Dayna finds repellent.

'Animals' tries to challenge viewers to consider whether the ends justify the means, as Justin tries to make sense of his work, prompting reflection on the ethical boundaries of scientific inquiry.

Moreover, the episode tries to shine a light on the intersection of ethics and military technology.

Justin's experiments were not solely motivated by scientific curiosity but by the Federation's desire to create intelligent animal servants for military purposes.

This raises additional moral questions about the use of animals in warfare and the ethical responsibilities of scientists involved in military research.

In essence, 'Animals' serves as a cautionary tale about the dangers of unchecked scientific ambition and the ethical dilemmas inherent in the pursuit of knowledge. It is somewhat sad therefore that the episode doesn't really work terribly well as a piece of entertainment.

By confronting viewers with the moral complexities of animal experimentation, the episode encourages us to critically examine the ethical implications of our actions and consider the ethical treatment of sentient beings.

What it probably needed was a climatic confrontation between Justin and Ogg, a *Frankenstein*-like scene of the monster killing his creator.

Teacher-student romance is another ethical issue this episode raises. Another ethical dilemma presented here revolves around Justin's romantic feelings towards Dayna, his former student.

The episode taps into the complexities of age gaps and power dynamics in relationships, particularly those between teachers and students. Justin's affection for Dayna raises pertinent questions about the appropriateness of such relationships and the ethical boundaries that should govern them.

The portrayal of Justin and Dayna's relationship highlights the inherent power imbalance between a teacher and their student. Justin, as Dayna's former mentor, holds a position of authority and influence over her, which complicates the dynamics of their romantic involvement.

This power dynamic raises concerns about consent and coercion, as well as the potential for exploitation in such relationships.

Additionally, the significant age gap between Justin and Dayna adds another layer of complexity to their romance. While love knows no bounds, the episode forces viewers to confront the ethical implications of romantic relationships characterized by substantial differences in age and life experience.

The episode prompts reflection on the

ethical responsibilities of individuals in positions of authority, particularly when it comes to navigating romantic entanglements with those under their guidance.

Ultimately, 'Animals' serves as a reminder of the ethical challenges inherent in teacher-student relationships.

What the episode probably needed was a third person in the scenes with Justin and Dayna. Avon, Vila or even Soolin might have served to be the voice of a third party, questioning the relationship, perhaps criticising the relationship with some subtle sarcasm.

By confronting viewers with the moral quandaries surrounding scientific experimentation on animals and teacher-student relationships, 'Animals' prompts reflection on the ethical responsibilities of individuals and institutions in positions of power.

It's a pity it reduces this potential to lengthy two hander scenes for Dayna and Justin. Josette Simon does her best to hold the attention of the viewer, but it is a tough task when the script is pedestrian and mediocre at times.

All in all, 'Animals' has potential and some potent themes and ideas behind it.

On the other hand, there is just not enough of Avon in this episode.

THE SLAVE COMPUTER'S MOST HUMBLE ASSESSMENT OF THE SITUATION:

6/10

HEADHUNTER

A killer robot, the final creation of Ensor's prize pupil Muller, is on the rampage in the base. Intent on total control of the universe, it needs Orac to fulfil its destiny. (VHS release summary)

Vila and Tarrant land on planet Pharos with a mission to bring Dr Muller, a renowned cyberneticist, on-board - a strategic move by Avon to strengthen their team.

However, things take an unexpected turn on the Scorpio when Muller exhibits aggressive behaviour towards an enigmatic box that Tarrant has in his possession.

In an attempt to control the situation, Vila confronts Muller but tragically ends up killing him with a wrench blow.

Muller's body is placed in a cryogenic capsule, but unfortunately, Scorpio's power and life support systems fails shortly after.

As the pair find themselves stuck in Xenon's orbit, Tarrant and Vila are saved from death by their comrades. However, Muller - who was presumed dead - has mysteriously vanished.

We soon discover the shocking truth that Muller is actually an unyielding android who murdered its creator.

To deceive everyone, it even went to the extreme of carrying around its creator's severed head. The head was worn on the android's neck and the machine was able to animate it to the extent it could speak.

Without the head, the android appears looking like a headless apparition of legend.

The robot stealthily makes its way through the base with a scheme to 'fuse' with Orac, banking on their united AI capabilities to render them all powerful and unbeatable.

The only possible deterrent could be what's inside the peculiar box— the actual intended head of the android.

Orac deduces the truth of the threat and is certain this headless android must be destroyed, or else humanity will be enslaved by this machine forever.

EXPLORING THE DUAL NATURE OF TECHNOLOGY

In the realm of science fiction television series, few have pondered the complexities and implications of technology as profoundly as *Blake's 7*.

The episode 'Headhunter' stands out as a tense and clever dramatization of humanity's relationship with artificial intelligence (AI) and the dilemmas it presents.

In 'Headhunter,' the crew encounters a formidable adversary: an advanced android posing as a man named Muller. This super android possesses a singular goal - to merge with the powerful supercomputer Orac and ascend to dominance over humanity.

'Headhunter' serves as a cautionary tale, dramatizing society's fears of AI surpassing human control and seeking to subjugate its creators. The Muller android's desire to merge with Orac symbolizes the potential for technology to evolve beyond our intentions and become a threat to our very existence.

It's the type of plot which would be a huge hit a few years later in James Cameron's film *Terminator* and the relentless android here is seen hunting for Orac and his human helpers in a similarly implacable manner.

Like rebel leader Avalon from season one's 'Project Avalon' and gunfighter Vinnie from season three's 'Death Watch', Muller is the latest use of the popular *Blake's 7* story trope of the person who turns out to be a cunningly disguised android menace.

It raises essential questions about the ethical boundaries of technological advancement and the responsibility we bear as creators. At what point are we creating our own destruction or downfall?

At the heart of the episode lies a compelling dichotomy regarding the use of technology as a tool for liberation or oppression.

Avon, ever the most pragmatic and morally ambiguous member of the rebel crew, sees the potential of harnessing the Muller android's power as a weapon against the Federation.

In his eyes, technology is a means to an end, a tool to be wielded in the pursuit of freedom and justice.

However, Avon's decision to utilize the android as a weapon against the Federation ultimately backfires, highlighting the inherent risks of playing with forces beyond our control.

Despite his intentions, Avon underestimates the complexity of the android's motives and the extent of its capabilities.

In the end, it is not the oppressive Federation that poses the greatest threat, but the unintended consequences of humanity's own creation.

The climax of 'Headhunter' serves as a sobering reminder of the double-edged nature of technology.

While it offers the promise of progress and empowerment, it also harbors the potential for destruction and subjugation. The decision to destroy the android represents a recognition of this inherent risk and a reaffirmation of humanity's agency in determining its own fate.

The humour is well placed to underscore the theme at the very end, too. Avon bitterly calling Tarrant a superstitious fool, holding them back with ignorance and fear. Orac counters by stating it is arrogance like Avon's which threatens them all.

Enraged, Avon snarls at Orac to 'shut up' and he sarcastically replies, 'yes...Master!'

It is funny but it also makes the point of the story and its theme very plain. Humans are the masters of their technology, but they could so easily see things turn the other way around and end up enslaved by their own creations. Dominance is precarious, fragile and power can be lost very easily.

In conclusion, 'Headhunter' stands as a thought-provoking exploration of the complex relationship between humanity and technology.

Through its compelling narrative and nuanced characters, it challenges viewers to confront the ethical dilemmas posed by AI and consider the consequences of our technological pursuits. It is one last Orac and Ensor based storyline and a welcome change of pace from the ongoing struggle with Servalan and the Federation.

Ultimately, it is a story which reminds us that the true measure of progress lies not in the advancement of technology itself, but in our ability to wield it responsibly for the betterment of humanity.

THE SLAVE COMPUTER'S MOST HUMBLE ASSESSMENT OF THE SITUATION:

10/10

ASSASSIN

At first glance the Federation transmission seems irrelevant. Then Scorpio's crew discover that Servalan is the Utiliser, Cancer is an infallible hired assassin and they are the five subjects. (VHS release summary)

The team from Scorpio sets course for the slave planet, Domo, armed with intel that Servalan has commissioned a feared assassin named 'Cancer' to wipe them out.

The details about this lethal hit man are scarce - his appearance remains a mystery and the only known fact about him is his impeccable track record.

Avon willingly gets himself enslaved with the intention of reaching Servalan before anyone else.

However, his plan falls short as Cancer has already vacated the planet. With assistance from a fellow slave, Nebrox, Avon manages to break free and locate Cancer's ship.

He and Tarrant then teleport themselves

aboard.

Cancer is discovered in the company of a young slave girl, Piri, and they successfully capture him.

Avon's strategy involves lying low for Servalan, assuming she'll show up to pay Cancer.

However, their plan backfires spectacularly when the assassin discloses their real identity, revealing that they've been ensnared in an intricate trap all along.

UNVEILING DECEPTION:

EXPLORING GENDER STEREOTYPES

Blake's 7 is often notable for its exploration of complex themes and characters. 'Assassin,' delves into the dynamics of gender stereotypes and deception, albeit with some hiccups along the way.

At the heart of 'Assassin' lies a fascinating premise: the unveiling of an assassin's true identity challenges conventional notions of gender and appearance.

As with season one's 'Mission to Destiny' and to an extent, season two's 'Voice from the Past', there is a sense of an Agatha Christie type mystery on a spaceship, with the unmasking of a hidden killer.

Like the popular game *Cluedo* or *Clue* as it is known in the USA, there is always a sense of anticipation of a victim or two, before the reveal that it was Sara in the flight deck with a mallet, Travis in a mask with a knife or, in this case, Piri in the prison cell with a crab.

Initially presenting us with the image of an implacable blonde man reminiscent of a *Terminator* archetype, the episode swiftly subverts expectations by revealing the true assassin—a woman.

This clever twist plays on the age-old adage that appearances can be deceiving, and it does so with an attempted exploration of gender roles.

The female assassin's guise as a helpless, weak, and sweet girl underscores the pervasive societal belief that femininity equates to vulnerability.

However, her transformation into a cold, calculating, and arrogant killer shatters these preconceptions, highlighting the multifaceted nature of female characters.

It's a commentary on the underestimated power of women and the dangers of underestimating individuals based on their gender.

Yet, despite the episode's commendable thematic exploration, it does stumble in its portrayal of the assassin character.

The initial depiction of the Terminator-like figure as a stand-in for the real assassin feels somewhat disjointed and fails to fully capitalize on the narrative's potential.

This awkward execution detracts from the episode's overall impact, likely leaving many viewers yearning for a more seamless integration of the central theme.

Nevertheless, 'Assassin' remains a compelling instalment in the *Blake's 7* series, offering viewers a thought-provoking journey through the complexities of gender perception and deception.

It serves as a timely reminder not to judge a book by its cover and challenges us to question our ingrained stereotypes and biases.

What lets it down is partly in the script. Piri is just too grotesquely pitiful and simpering to 'make a big impression on Tarrant'. Her alter ego is too cartoonish and far too much like a pantomime 'wicked witch' villainess to convince as a brilliant assassin.

Considering the series was well loved for

the undeniable humanity which underscored the villainy of characters such as Servalan and Travis, this was a bridge too far, a lurch from the sublime to the ridiculous.

Guest star Caroline Holdaway is perhaps an unfair target for criticism. On the one hand, she is neither lovable enough to win over Tarrant with her simpering and whining, nor sane and level-headed enough to convince as a mastermind super-assassin who could outwit the likes of Avon.

But in fairness to the actress, she does deliver a very committed and two sided performance in a somewhat thankless role.

While it may not rank among the series' best episodes, its thematic richness and insightful commentary make it a worthwhile addition to the *Blake's 7* watch list.

There is also the guest character of Nebrox, played by Richard Hurndall in a red cloak that makes him look a lot like first *Doctor Who* William Hartnell crica 'The Romans'. He is a definite highlight of the episode.

Not only did fans find him reminiscent of

the first Doctor, so did producer John Nathan Turner who promptly hired him to play the first Doctor in 'The Five Doctors' for *Doctor Who's* 20th anniversary special in 1983.

Nebrox is so much like the first Doctor, he adds an additional layer of enjoyment to the episode.

Another highlight is Avon allowing himself to be captured and sold off as a slave.

Possibly tapping deliberately into Paul Darrow's growing status as a television sex symbol, he's auctioned off with a very funny sales pitch which includes the idea that Avon can put in a full day's work for his new slave-owner and still have plenty of energy left for any additional duties he may be asked to perform in the evenings.

The idea of Servalan bidding on Avon is simply the stuff of television gold. Pearce seems to be having a whale of a time in these scenes, too.

In conclusion, 'Assassin' is a fun if not completely satisfying episode which entertains on the whole and invites us to reconsider our assumptions about gender and appearance, urging us to look beyond the surface and recognize the true depth of character within each individual.

It may stumble along the way, with some clunky scenes and some over the top acting, not to mention some poor production standards, but its tentative exploration of societal norms and expectations, as well as its playful use of Servalan and Avon, ensures its lasting relevance.

THE SLAVE COMPUTER'S MOST HUMBLE ASSESSMENT OF THE SITUATION:

7/10

GAMES

Feldon crystals - the most powerful energy source in the galaxy, only found on the planet Mecron. One man alone supervises the mining there for the Federation - Belkov, the master gameplayer. The temptation proved too much for Avon and now Scorpio's crew must play along with Belkov to stand a chance of surviving at all. (VHS release summary)

Belkov, a man with a penchant for intricate games of skill, is in charge of a Feldon crystal extraction operation on Mecron II for Servalan. However, the truth is that he's swindling her by secretly keeping a significant portion of the crystal haul to himself.

These crystals are not ordinary; they possess unlimited energy potential, and their value surpasses even that of diamonds.

Servalan smells a rat in Belkov's actions and warns him of dire consequences, but only after extracting information about the crystal's location.

Meanwhile, Belkov reaches out to Avon with a tempting offer - the stolen crystal for his rescue.

But Avon, ever the sceptic, senses that Belkov might be using this rescue mission as a ruse to blame the Scorpio crew for the missing crystal.

GAMES, SET AND MATCH

'Games' presents the themes of fun, games, gambling, and the pursuit of power.

Set against the backdrop of a dangerous planet, the episode delves into the folly of greed and the deceptive allure of power.

At the heart of the episode is a jolly man who introduces an element of playfulness amidst the perilous circumstances faced by the protagonists.

His interactions with a computer, which appears more like a friend and lover than a mere machine, add layers of intrigue and mystique to the narrative.

Through their seemingly innocent games, the true stakes of life and death emerge, blurring the lines between amusement and existential threat.

As the heroes navigate through a series of challenges and tests, the viewer is drawn into a game of survival.

Each trial presents an opportunity for the characters to showcase their wit, cunning, and resilience. Tarrant gets to use his skill as a space pilot, Soolin enjoys the challenge of facing herself on a screen in a quick draw shooting contest and Vila's genius for opening doors and locks comes to the fore as well.

However, beneath the surface allure of the games lies a deeper truth – the pursuit of power and wealth is often an illusion, leading only to disappointment and disillusionment. It's the type of theme that constantly gives *Blake's 7* the feeling of a savvy show for intelligent viewers. It may seem somewhat cynical at times, yet it is hard to deny the integrity of a series which draws inspiration from George Orwell.

The climax of the episode unveils the ultimate deception: the crystals of great power and value, which the characters have been striving to obtain, turn out to be nothing more than worthless fakes.

In this moment of revelation, the facade of greed is shattered, exposing the emptiness of material pursuits.

Guest star Stratford Johns, famous and popular for his long running role as a police officer in British TV's *Softly, Softly: Taskforce,* and later to appear on *Doctor Who* as Monarch in 'Four to Doomsday', brings his considerable screen presence and jolly personality to the character of Belkov.

His interplay with Servalan is particularly good. 'They found my survival quite miraculous,' he says of the natives on the planet, referring to a ruse he pulled to manipulate them into thinking he had divine protection from death.

Servalan replies, witheringly, 'Your survival is getting more miraculous by the minute...'

All in all, 'Games' serves as a reminder of the dangers of unchecked ambition and the pitfalls of chasing after hollow rewards.

For in the game of life, it is not the prizes we accumulate but the experiences we cherish that truly define our journey.

For our heroes, the journey was perilous and would only get more treacherous from here.

THE

SLAVE COMPUTER'S

MOST HUMBLE

ASSESSMENT OF THE

SITUATION:

8/10

SAND

With Tarrant and Servalan held captive by vampire sand, stranded together on the green planet of Virn, and Scorpio trapped by the planet's atmosphere, Avon must take drastic action to save the crew. (VHS release summary)

Servalan lands on Virn, a planet peculiarly blanketed with green sand, to investigate the mysterious disappearance of a Federation research team.

This team vanished five years ago shortly after discovering a substance with exceptional energy capabilities.

The team from Scorpio trail her to the planet, intrigued by her actions. Upon Servalan's arrival, she faces a setback as her ship malfunctions and her ally, Investigator Reeve, betrays her.

She is left isolated until she crosses paths with Tarrant who had teleported down with Dayna to monitor her movements.

The duo is forced to cooperate for their survival, seeking refuge in a bunker to shield themselves from the green sand - an entity that appears to possess life and intelligence.

Concurrently, an unusual energy storm incapacitates Scorpio, rendering it incapable of executing a rescue mission.

This concept of alien life is a remarkable example of the rare but intriguing way the series incorporates aliens into the narrative. It makes for a striking contrast to the aliens who regularly populate the show's stable mate *Doctor Who*.

Blakes 7's aliens are often humanoid, quite often bald and occasionally dwarfish or blue.

But the really interesting notions, which *Doctor Who* could've borrowed inspiration from, was such things as the moving, living, parasitic green sands of the episode 'Sand', the living cloud of aggressive enzymes which invades and horrifically eats the Liberator, the dead alien who tries to recreate herself by absorbing Cally and even the largely unseen, until a quick glimpse at the end, of the Thaarn.

Then there's the unknown aliens who unleash a virus via a corpse which sits up and chokes a man in 'Killer', the Andromedan aliens who are really only implied with a green glow and a patch of slime and other quivering stuff and generally are represented as dopplegangers of humans.

By playing down the aliens as a physical presence and playing up human evil, *Blake's 7* often accomplishes a lot on a very small budget.

It's something *Doctor Who* did rarely, but a good comparison might be Jon Pertwee's much loved season 7, where the four serials focus on humans like Stahlman, Carrington and Dr Quinn and the monsters are enigmatic figures in space suits, window dummies or men whose skin is turning green and infected.

Perhaps if *Doctor Who* had tried to do more of *Blakes 7*'s approach to aliens, we could've had more seasons like season 7.

And now, come to think of it, that living sand would've been great as a menace on *Doctor Who*.

SAND TRAPS

Tannith Lee returns two writing for the series and once again the difference in having a woman writing an episode as well as someone who was an accomplished science fiction author and novelist makes a huge difference to the style, content and quality of the script.

The episode begins with poetry and a theme of love and romance runs throughout the episode.

The writer goes to great lengths to focus on the character of Servalan. Her interactions with Steven Yardley's swaggering and self-confident character Reeve, early on in the episode, serve to demonstrate that she is in her own words a 'unique' character.

She is completely unlike other women and definitely not someone to be messed with or taken lightly by any man or indeed woman.

The latter half of the episode in which she is trapped with Tarrant reveals another side of her as it becomes obvious that we are about to learn the secret to her character's motivation and personality.

It seems that when she was young she met the love of her life only to lose him and the empty void he left behind meant that she was forced to turn to something else to compensate for his loss.

Power has become a drug to which she is addicted, and it has become the substitute for love in her life. The final moments in the episode are genuinely moving and deeply emotional and the episode affords actress Jacqueline Pearce the opportunity to give her greatest acting performance in the series.

Once again the ideas behind the story have been very well worked out before the script was written.

The concept of a planet where the sand is alive and capable of moving and the notion that this living sand needs to keep the strongest man as well as at least one woman alive as breeding stock so they can feed upon their bodies is a superb one for both science fiction horror and for character development.

As with the writers previous script there are a large number of small moments which give us new insights into the regular characters and make this episode a rich experience.

There is also some clever humour in the script.

It is quite hilarious when Soolin and Dayna realise that Avon has been chosen as the dominant male.

Although the character of Vila does not have a lot to do in the episode, his character is used well as the malicious alien sand attempts to kill him.

'Sand' also represents an impressive attempt to present a memorable and distinctive alien planet in the series with the green planet of Virn.

Most of the 52 episodes focus on Earth-like planets which resemble gravel quarries or forests and most of them are almost interchangeable with each other.

However the planet Virn with its green sands and starry night skies is punctuated by lightning bolts and eerie mist.

It joins the icy planet from project Avalon and the watery world of Aristo as one of the few truly vivid and memorable alien planets ever depicted in the series.

All in all this is an outstanding story and an exceptional effort has been made to bring it to life on screen.

HUMANITY IN BLAKE'S 7:

EXPLORING TANITH LEE'S 'SAND'

Certain *Blake's 7* episodes stand out, not just for their thrilling plots, but for their nuanced exploration of characters. 'Sand,' penned by the gifted woman author Tanith Lee, is one such gem that delves into the depths of its characters amidst the backdrop of a strange, green planet of living sand.

From the onset, 'Sand' captivates with its eerie setting, drawing viewers into a world where the very ground beneath their feet is alive. But beyond the surface allure lies a rich character study, particularly focusing on Servalan.

Lee's script masterfully humanizes Servalan, peeling back the layers of her character to reveal vulnerabilities and complexities that challenge traditional notions of good and evil.

While Servalan has often been portrayed as the cold, calculating antagonist in previous episodes, 'Sand' offers a glimpse into her psyche, showcasing the emotional scars that have shaped her into the formidable figure she is.

Central to Servalan's character arc in 'Sand' is her encounter with Tarrant. Through their interactions, we witness a rare moment of vulnerability from Servalan, as her icy facade begins to crack under the weight of her past.

We learn that power, for Servalan, has become a substitute for love, a coping mechanism born out of the loss of her true love.

What makes 'Sand' truly compelling is its willingness to blur the lines between hero and villain, painting Servalan as a human, flawed character worthy of empathy and understanding.

In doing so, the episode adopts a film noir aesthetic, where moral ambiguity reigns and characters are not simply black and white, but shades of grey.

Furthermore, 'Sand' subverts traditional gender dynamics by placing a female character at the forefront of the narrative, allowing Servalan to transcend the typical confines of female villainy and emerge as a fully realized, multifaceted character.

But unlike 'Assassin' and the over the top portrayal of Piri and her alter ego Cancer, 'Sand' is scripted with real skill and is highly effective in exploring the duality and grey shades of Servalan.

Tanith Lee is on top form here, the character work is sublime, and Jacqueline Pearce is able to make complete sense of Servalan at last, leaving us with the lasting impression of a woman whose cold, ruthless path in life has been a tragedy, not a triumph.

Servalan is just one more example of the painful emptiness of life for those human beings who are unlucky enough to be born into this world of the future, to inhabit the totalitarian society of the Terran Federation. In her own way, she is just as tragic as our heroes.

In some respects the theme here is reminiscent of Shakespeare's *Macbeth* where power is a substitute for Macbeth and his wife as they are a childless couple. Servalan is very much in the tradition of Lady Macbeth and the notion that she has acquired power as a substitute for love is fitting for her character.

The episode also challenges our perceptions of the heroes, too.

Tarrant's role adds depth to the narrative, forcing viewers to question their preconceived notions of good and bad characters.

In conclusion, Tanith Lee's 'Sand' is a testament to the power of science fiction to explore complex themes and characters with depth and nuance.

Through its literate script and captivating storytelling, 'Sand' invites viewers to reconsider their understanding of morality and empathy, leaving a lasting impression long after the credits roll.

In the midst of the unfolding drama on the green planet of living sand, 'Sand' takes an unexpected turn when rebel Tarrant's act of mercy towards their enemy, Servalan, is revealed to his comrades aboard the Scorpio.

Tarrant's decision to show compassion

towards Servalan, driven by his own sympathy for her vulnerabilities, thrusts him into the role of a traitor in the eyes of his friends.

This revelation adds another layer of tension and conflict within the episode, as the crew grapples with the betrayal of their own principles and the trust they once placed in Tarrant.

The fallout from this revelation not only tests the bonds of camaraderie among the crew but also forces them to confront their own moral convictions in the face of Tarrant's unexpected compassion for their enemy.

THE SLAVE COMPUTER'S MOST HUMBLE ASSESSMENT OF THE SITUATION:

10/10

GOLD

When Keiller, the purser of the cruise ship Space Princess, makes Scorpio's crew a lucrative offer, Avon is loath to refuse. After all, who could resist the temptation to hide 17 billion in gold, even if it does belong to Servalan? (VHS release summary)

Keiller, a familiar face from Avon's past, lets him in on a covert operation involving the transfer of gold from planet Zerok to the Federation.

This is all happening through a passenger liner known as the Space Princess. Keiller has his eyes set on this gold and intends to snatch it away, but he can't do it alone.

He proposes a deal to Avon and his team - assist him with this daring heist and they'll get their share of the treasure.

Nonetheless, the plan requires retrieving the gold from Zerok before it's transformed into 'black gold'—an atomic variant that holds no value until it's reverted back to its original state through a coded computer procedure.

Keiller spearheads the intrusion into the Zerok facility. However, they walk right into a trap as the guards are already alerted—thanks to Servalan's cunning setup.

Avon has made a bold decision to intercept the upcoming black gold shipment directly from the Princess and then resell it to Servalan.

'Gold' is a pretty decent episode.

The main guest star, Roy Kinear, is a comedy legend, of course, well remembered these days for playing the long suffering father of snobby posh diva Veruca Salt in the classic movie *Willy Wonka and the Chocolate Factory*.

One of the funny things here is the way Vila stays behind and Avon decides to convince Keiller that the unseen Vila is some kind of ruthless hardened criminal type that Keiller should be very wary of upsetting.

Also amusing is Tarrant posing as a dim-witted passenger on the space liner as part of their sting operation. It's a nice chance to see the lighter side of actor Steven Pacey.

Peter Tuddenham almost steals the show as Orac actually laughs at his human comrades as he delivers his final dose of bad news to them. Orac seems quite tickled by the extent of their folly.

And the sight of Avon losing it at the end, laughing like a loon, almost hysterical at the irony of their latest brutal humiliation, is really quite something to behold.

GOLDEN THOUGHTS

BY KEN DEEP

'Gold' is a straightforward space caper. A heist story done with as much style as a series D budget would allow.

There's some wonderful model work with the space cruise ship. The tin trays decorating its safe room walls can be forgiven with a guest turn by movie star Roy Kinnear.

The guest casting of Kinnear allows this episode to punch above its weight. He turns in a compelling performance as a high level Federation agent masquerading as a supposedly underpaid purser.

Although he has no hesitation to kill, it's difficult to picture him as a ruthless killer employed on Servalan's staff.

He's smarmy, for sure, but panics easily when his life is in danger. Kinnear shines when he plays midlife crisis Keiller as a man ostensibly without retirement savings. There's an understated desperation that makes his performance purely cinematic and I love it.

The episode ends with a rendezvous with Servalan, a shock and surprise to no one at this point.

She turns up on a deserted planet with a handful of her Federation guards on some kind of beach buggy. This anachronism might be distracting except that the dialog between Paul Darrow and Jacqueline Pearce is delicious.

The caper falls apart when it turns out that the booty our heroes acquired becomes worthless. Soolin's cool professionalism is tested and results in her outburst 'We risked our lives to make Servalan rich!'

Not a particularly surprising twist is made enjoyable however by Avon's hearty laugh.

It's nice to see some of the dystopian darkness return to the *Blake's 7* universe. The passengers aboard the Space Princess are again drugged, reminiscent of the universe seen more often in series A.

It feels like everyone is up to no good. The crew are money hungry, Keiller can't be trusted, the Federation are drugging the population, and even seemingly innocent characters pose a risk.

That threat is skilfully on display when Keiller shoots the cruise ship's doctor. Everything you might need to encapsulate *Blake's 7* is expressed by Keiller in his brief line "everyone's dangerous" and he was right, for once.

FOOL'S GOLD

ANOTHER PERSPECTIVE

This episode is interesting for a number of reasons. If the story was purely a space heist like 'Harvest of Kairos the previous season then 'Gold' would depict our heroes as simple criminals.

However, in a typically clever *Blake's 7* twist, it turns out that Avon has been using this heist as an opportunity to get to Servalan, whom he suspects is behind the whole thing.

As with almost all of the episodes in the fourth season, the concepts and ideas behind the story are very well worked out.

The idea of a gold planet that uses gold to trade with planets which do not yet use the Federation credit system is good, the idea that a man who is in charge of security wants to work with Avon, who he knows from the past, is also good and the idea that the gold is being smuggled under the noses of pirates and raiders passenger liner is also clever. The notion that the gold is being molecularly changed into a black substance to make it useless to thieves is an interesting idea, too.

Overall it adds up to a good premise, leading to a fairly strong story and the whole thing is pretty well executed.

The irony that Servalan has been enriched by our heroes' actions and they have ended up with nothing, leads to a very interesting moment for the character of Avon, breaking out in hysterical laughter, taking his usual habit of grinning or smiling in the face of bad news to a whole new level.

This moment invites serious comparison with the character of Walter White in *Breaking Bad who* breaks into hysterical laughter at the end of the episode 'Crawl Space' when he realises he is completely screwed for deeply ironic reasons.

It's a testament to the acting skill of Paul Darrow that he pulls off this moment very convincingly and it raises questions about his character's sanity and mental stability.

Just how far is he gone to the edge and how much of a toll is the whole thing taking on his mind?

UNVEILING THE PERILS OF GREED AND BETRAYAL IN 'GOLD'

Some episodes are content to just be harmless fun. 'Gold,' is an episode which is looking at a very human failing, greed, yet also finds time and space for levity and fun.

Set against the backdrop of Blake's 7's dystopian galactic society, 'Gold' follows our band of rebels on a daring mission to steal a cache of gold.

Terry Nation might have envisaged the seven robbing from the rich to give to the poor, but Avon is no Robin Hood. He has much darker intentions in mind.

Fuelled by promises of untold riches, our protagonists are seduced by the allure of wealth, each driven by their own desires and motivations.

From his introduction in 'Space Fall', where he was revealed to have been involved in a plot to defraud the Federation banking system, Avon has had a complex relationship with greed, seeing wealth as 'the only reality'.

Encouraged by an 'old friend' to seize the opportunity for financial gain, Avon's ambition blinds him to the dangers that lie ahead. Or does it? Here he is fishing for more than just the freedom money can buy, he is risking his life for a chance to kill Servalan, something which ties in well with the dark statement he made at the conclusion of 'Traitor'.

His folly ultimately leads to tragedy, as his friend falls victim to the machinations of their mutual enemy, Servalan.

As the plot unfolds, it becomes clear that the pursuit of gold is not without its consequences.

Avon's old friend comes to a sticky ending which serves as a cautionary tale, a stark reminder of the price one pays for succumbing to the temptations of greed.

In a world where gold holds sway over hearts and minds, the true cost of wealth is laid bare for all to see.

Our heroes' quest for riches ultimately proves to be a hollow endeavour, as they come to realize they've been chasing a hollow dream.

In conclusion, 'Gold' stands as a testament to the perils of greed and betrayal and is one of the better episodes of the fourth season.

THE SLAVE COMPUTER'S MOST HUMBLE ASSESSMENT OF THE SITUATION:

8/10

ORBIT

Egrorian, famed genius and scientist, has created the lethal tachyon funnel, a weapon powerful enough to blast the Federation out of the galaxy and he's willing to do a deal with Avon and the crew. It would be a simple exchange: the ultimate weapon for the ultimate computer - Orac. (VHS release summary)

A rogue scientist, Egrorian, beckons Avon to the inhospitable planet of Malodar with a proposition too enticing to decline. Accompanied by Vila, Avon descends onto the planet and encounters Egrorian and his aide, Pinder.

Egrorian showcases his 'Tachyon Funnel', a formidable weapon capable of obliterating anything in the cosmos by utilizing super-dense stellar matter. The only thing he demands in exchange is Orac. Avon, albeit hesitantly, contemplates the trade. However, he later returns with a counterfeit Orac and successfully tricks Egrorian into handing over the weapon system.

Servalan is the mastermind orchestrating

the transfer covertly. As Avon and Vila are on their way back to Scorpio, Egrorian uncovers that the swapped Orac is a counterfeit.

Yet, he has manipulated the shuttle to crash. Avon is now confronted with the tough decision of discarding both the weapon and Vila to lighten the ship's weight enough to achieve escape velocity.

This episode takes its inspiration from none other than Tom Godwin's 'The Cold Equations', which delves deeply into the theme of sacrifice. The narrative revolves around Marilyn, a young stowaway on a spaceship, oblivious to the fact that her added weight is depleting the spaceship's fuel reserves.

This situation forces the pilot into a challenging predicament as he must ensure that he reaches planet Woden to deliver crucial supplies for its inhabitants.

'Orbit' is the episode where we really see a simple, tightly focused plot from Robert Holmes, and it is a revelation.

'Orbit' contains a favourite piece of dialog

in *Blake's 7* and probably one of the greatest ever from the pen of Bob Holmes. When Egrorian first meets Avon and Vila, there is a very clever exchange.

Egrorian: Surprisingly, you don't look like the ruthless desperadoes of legend. But you have, of course, killed a great many people.

Avon: Only in the pursuit of liberty.

Egrorian: O Liberty! O Liberty! What crimes are committed in your name! Do you know the source?

Avon: No.

Egrorian: No, why should you? Natural leaders are rarely encumbered with intelligence. Greed, egotism, animal cunning, and viciousness are the important attributes. Qualities I detect in you in admirably full measure.

Avon: I didn't come here to be... flattered.

As funny as this is, it foreshadows the idea of Avon committing a terrible crime in the name of his own liberty and survival.

THE DEPTHS OF SPACE:

AVON'S MORAL DILEMMA IN THE UNIVERSE OF BLAKE'S 7

In the vast expanse of space, where the laws of survival reign supreme, writer Robert Holmes crafts a masterful narrative that pushes the boundaries of loyalty and betrayal in 'Orbit'. This is one of the best Blake's 7 episodes ever made and arguably a contender for the title of best episode of the series.

In a pivotal moment aboard the shuttle spacecraft, Avon finds himself confronted with an impossible choice that tests the limits of his morality and survival instincts.

As the weight of their predicament bears down upon them, the Orac computer calculates the harsh reality: the ship is too heavy, and drastic measures must be taken to ensure their survival.

It's an intersection of Orac's emotionless computer logic and Avon's totally unsentimental, brutally realistic outlook. In a chilling demonstration of his pragmatic nature, Avon determines that the only solution is to jettison excess weight, even if it means sacrificing his friend, Vila, to the cold expanse of space.

Vila overhears and hides. One of the fascinating things here is that Avon is cautious in hunting Vila, as though he expects Vila to make a fight of it, possibly attempting to ambush him.

Yet Vila, apparently seeing Avon as a man against whom he stands no chance whatsoever, simply chooses to hide in a wall cavity and wait it out.

The moment when Avon realises what he must do to survive and the sight of Vila, dripping with cold sweat and curled into an almost-foetal position like a frightened child, make for remarkably emotional and tense drama.

Robert Holmes orchestrates a harrowing sequence that encapsulates the moral complexity of Avon's character, drawing viewers into a sequence which asks them to see both men's perspectives.

The scene unfolds with palpable dread as Avon hunts Vila, gun in hand and tries to coax him out with lies and pleas for help.

Vila seems to know the grim reality of their situation. At last he sees the way Avon sees things. It was there in the death of Dr Plaxton in 'Stardrive', but here its full implications hit home.

Avon is torn between the bonds of friendship and the instinct for self-preservation.

He is choosing his own life even at the cost of ending Vila's. We might feel anger or even hatred toward him, yet his logic stands: both are doomed, but one could survive.

In this brilliant display of human drama, the episode navigates the murky waters of morality, challenging viewers to confront the uncomfortable truths lurking beneath the surface.

Through Avon's actions, we are forced to grapple with the harsh realities of survival, where loyalty is a luxury few can afford, and betrayal is the currency of survival.

As Avon solves the problem of the

weighed-down ship, finding a few specs of neutron material embedded in a block of plastic, Vila survives the ordeal, but the fact remains Avon was apparently willing to kill him.

Avon jokes at the end that Vila is always safe with him, but it's a very dark jest.

The weight of Avon's cold blooded decision hangs heavy in the air.

And in that moment, Robert Holmes leaves us with a question – in a universe governed by the laws of survival, how far would we go to save ourselves, and at what cost to our humanity?

Actor Paul Darrow's perspective on Avon's character adds a fascinating layer to the discussion of 'Orbit', suggesting that Avon's actions are not driven by ruthlessness but by a stark realism shaped by the harsh environment of the universe in which he exists.

Darrow's argument challenges viewers to reconsider their interpretation of Avon's decisions, framing them not as acts of betrayal but as pragmatic responses to the unforgiving nature of their circumstances. 'If you were in the same situation, maybe you would do the same', Darrow suggests.

Indeed, Avon's relentless pursuit of survival and self-preservation forces us to confront uncomfortable questions about our own capacity for moral compromise in the face of adversity.

Would we, like Avon, be willing to make the same difficult choices to ensure our own survival and that of our comrades?

In a universe governed by the laws of survival, where every decision carries weight and consequences, it's a thought-provoking question that resonates deeply with viewers.

Paul Darrow's portrayal of Avon as a character driven, not by malice, but by a cold, calculated realism, challenges us to empathize with his plight, to see beyond the surface of his actions and understand the underlying motivations that drive him.

In doing so, we are compelled to confront the uncomfortable truth that in certain circumstances, we may all be capable of making similar choices.

It's the same situation that was raised in 'Stardrive', where Avon's impeccable logic concluded that Dr Plaxton was dead no matter what he did or did not do, so he simply took the decision to ensure her loss was the only one.

In the end, Paul Darrow's perspective on Avon's character invites us to re-examine our understanding of morality and survival in the context of *Blake's 7*, reminding us that the line between heroism and villainy is often blurred.

Challenging narratives and morally complex characters like Avon in *Blake's 7* are not necessarily rare in television, but they certainly stand out amidst a landscape often dominated by more straightforward storytelling.

While many TV shows opt for clear-cut heroes and villains, series like *Blake's 7* push the boundaries by exploring themes of morality, power dynamics, and the human condition in more nuanced and thought-provoking ways.

Television has seen a rise in complex storytelling in recent years, with shows like

Breaking Bad, *Game of Thrones*, and *The Sopranos* captivating audiences with morally ambiguous protagonists and intricate plotlines.

These series challenge viewers to engage with difficult themes and confront uncomfortable truths, pushing the medium beyond mere entertainment and into the realm of art.

However, while challenging narratives may not be the norm, they have a long history in television, with shows like *The Twilight Zone*, and *Twin Peaks* paving the way for more daring and innovative storytelling.

These series demonstrate the power of television to provoke thought, spark conversation, and inspire introspection.

In this regard, while challenging television may not be the most common, it remains a vital and impactful part of the medium, offering audiences a unique opportunity to engage with provocative ideas and explore the depths of the human psyche.

And in an era of ever-expanding content options, classic and daring series like

Blake's 7 serve as a reminder of the enduring power of television to challenge, inspire, and entertain.

With Avon's moral dilemma and the gripping narrative surrounding his decision to sacrifice his friend, Vila, 'Orbit' stands as a highlight of the final season of *Blake's 7*.

As the series nears its final end, the tension and drama reach new heights. Avon emerges not as a mere character but as a symbol of the human capacity for both heroism and villainy.

'Orbit' serves as a poignant reminder of the series' enduring legacy, its ability to captivate, challenge, and provoke thought long after the credits have rolled.

And in this, we find the true essence of great storytelling, a journey that leaves an indelible mark on the hearts and minds of its audience, long after the final curtain falls.

On the other hand, no review of 'Orbit' would be complete without one criticism. The prop for the Tachyon Funnel leaves a lot to be desired.

Little more than a portable television monitor and some vacuum hoses in a frame on wheels, it looks like something a school teacher wheeled out in 1980 to show a classroom of children an educational video.

Having said that, it performs its function well enough and cannot take away from the impact of this otherwise brilliant episode.

THE SLAVE COMPUTER'S MOST HUMBLE ASSESSMENT OF THE SITUATION:

10/10

WARLORD

With their Pylene-50 pacification programme going from strength to strength, the Federation's expansion continues relentlessly. In desperation Avon calls a conference of all the non allied planets. United they could effectively manage all the necessary anti-toxin. But their shaky alliance hinges on the mighty Zukan, and it is uncertain where his true loyalties lie. (VHS release summary)

Avon convenes a gathering on Xenon involving the five most influential groups opposing the Federation. Among these members is Zukan, who hails from planet Betafarl and holds a leadership position. Unknown to others, he is covertly in alliance with Servalan. He has compromised the security of the base by planting explosives and releasing a lethal radioactive virus intended to eliminate any survivors.

After Zukan leaves, the bombs go off. However, he's unaware that his daughter Zeeona, who happens to be Tarrant's girlfriend, remained on the base. To add to the drama, Servalan betrays Zukan by planting a bomb on his ship which sends it spiraling out of control.

On the planet Betafarl, Avon and Soolin are in a race against time to rescue their companions back on Xenon. Their only glimmer of hope lies in aiding Zukan first, as he alone possesses the knowledge to halt the deadly virus.

This episode marks the final episode featuring Jacqueline Pearce in the role of Servalan.

BETRAYAL AND CONSEQUENCES:

In the tumultuous universe of *Blake's 7*, alliances are fragile, and betrayal carries a heavy price. The episode 'Warlord' delves into these themes with gripping intensity, showcasing the complexities of rebellion, loyalty, and the devastating consequences of treachery.

At the heart of 'Warlord' is Zukan, a rebel leader reminiscent of the enigmatic Blake himself. Like Blake, Zukan commands loyalty and inspires hope among his followers. In many ways, Zukan is a mirror opposite of Blake, a man who appears to be a genuine ally whom Avon can depend upon in a final fight against the Federation, only to betray them, a move that ultimately leads to the tragic death of his own daughter.

This betrayal serves as a stark reminder of the moral ambiguity that permeates the struggle for freedom and power. It also reminds us again of the fear of betrayal which is at the core of Kerr Avon's persona and has been a key element of *Blake's 7* since Dev Tarrant betrayed the rebels on Earth in 'The Way Back'.

The emotional impact of losing his daughter weighs heavily on Zukan, haunting him with her image and the face of Servalan, who double-crosses him.

Zukan, mirroring Avon's pragmatic logic from 'Orbit' saves himself by ejecting his pilot into space when Servalan plants a bomb in their ship.

His grief and guilt add layers of complexity to his character, as he grapples with the consequences of his actions and the betrayal that has torn his family apart. Like Servalan herself, Zukan is no comic strip evil villain, but a three dimensional character who has simply chosen to side with the Federation and regretted it.

The episode masterfully highlights the price of treachery, illustrating how betrayal not only fractures alliances but also shatters lives and trust irreparably. Zukan's anguish serves as a poignant reminder of the human cost of war and the toll it takes on those caught in its crossfire.

'Warlord' foreshadows future conflicts within the series, particularly the strained relationship between Avon and Blake.

Avon's experience of feeling betrayed by someone he once trusted echoes Zukan's betrayal, laying the groundwork for the gripping tension that unfolds in the season finale.

As viewers are drawn deeper into the intricate web of alliances and deceit, 'Warlord' becomes a poignant reminder of the precarious nature of power and the moral complexities inherent in the fight for freedom.

It challenges viewers to confront the harsh realities of betrayal and the lasting impact it leaves on individuals and societies alike.

In conclusion, 'Warlord' stands as a compelling exploration of betrayal, sacrifice, and the fragile nature of alliances.

Through its compelling narrative and rich character development, it leaves an indelible impression on viewers, offering a thought-provoking reflection on the price of treachery in the pursuit of justice and liberation.

In this episode, Servalan makes her final appearance, where she kills Zukan. Zukan dies with her haunting face in his mind, tormenting him. In the next episode, Avon reveals that Zukan was standing in as a figurehead for another person, which is revealed to be Blake. This suggests that Zukan serves as a substitute for Blake.

The fact that Zukan is an ersatz Blake adds a certain resonance to Servalan's killing of him. It's as if we're witnessing how she might have defeated Blake if he had been the one Avon had turned to. Of course, Blake wouldn't betray his friends; he would have been pretending to work for Servalan in a similar scenario.

The idea of him in Zukan's place, finally defeated by Servalan, is an interesting one, as she would not actually appear in the next episode.

Instead, the final episode would revisit the faceless authoritarian power that Blake initially rebelled against in 'The Way Back.' It featured the nameless men in helmets who gunned down the rebels he encountered in the old tunnels outside the dome city on Earth. Therefore, the final episode would bring the series full circle.

THE SLAVE COMPUTER'S MOST HUMBLE ASSESSMENT OF THE SITUATION:

8/10

BLAKE

With the Xenon base destroyed and the fledgling alliance floundering, Avon must find another figurehead to take up the cause. Inevitably it is time to set a course for the lawless Gauda Prime to renew an old acquaintance. (VHS release summary)

Concerned that the Federation might have discovered the location of Xenon base, the Scorpio crew takes decisive action to demolish its remnants. Subsequently, Avon discloses his contemplation about identifying a new leader for their resistance - someone who could garner unanimous support.

He firmly believes that Blake is the ideal candidate for this role.

Orac has a strong hunch that Blake is still breathing and has pinpointed his location to the once anarchic planet of Gauda Prime.

Upon their arrival, Scorpio faces an assault from patrol ships, compelling it to land. Tarrant remains on board to steady the ship while the rest of the crew teleports down to the planet's surface.

In the meantime, Blake, who is not dead but masquerading as a bounty hunter, saves Tarrant from the wreckage and takes him back to their base.

Once there, he discovers that Tarrant is a member of Avon's rebellion group. He insinuates to Tarrant that his intention is to betray them to the Federation for a reward.

However, Tarrant manages to escape without understanding that Blake's actions were merely a test of his allegiance.

Tarrant encounters Avon and the rest of the crew, leading to a tense confrontation with Blake. Just as Blake is about to persuade Avon of his loyalty, a tragic twist occurs - Avon impulsively shoots and kills him.

In an unexpected turn of events, they are ambushed by a battalion of Federation soldiers who ruthlessly gun down everyone except for Avon.

Avon, in an act of sheer defiance, does not yield but instead towers over Blake's lifeless form.

With a smirk playing on his lips, he hoists his firearm aloft.

As the screen fades to black and the end credits roll in, the only sound piercing the silence is that of relentless gunfire.

His fate is left a mystery - an utterly tantalizing enigma with no resolution.

NOTABLE MOMENTS

Tarrant's miraculous escape from death:

It is set out that Tarrant looks to have been killed when Scorpio crash landed. However, he turns out to be alive. His miraculous survival misleads us into believing we're going to see things turn out okay. But no, Boucher is being darkly ironic here. Tarrant's survival is actually a terrible thing. It sets a chain of events in motion which have disastrous consequences as he is found by Blake.

Soolin's backstory:

Soolin's backstory is well-written, evoking empathy for her and helping us understand her motivations. Glynis Barber delivers it powerfully, showcasing her talent. She is an underrated actress and her character shines here. 'For a home you need a family and mine were murdered.' This is an interesting development on her introduction in 'Rescue' where we learn she killed the man who taught her to use a gun.

Avon's folly is about finding Blake again:

Avon appears to harbor a secret desire to locate Blake. However, this quest for Blake is his Achilles' heel, a folly that ultimately results in his downfall. Searching for Blake nearly cost him his life in 'Terminal' and led to the loss of the Liberator.

Despite this, he repeats the same mistake, with even graver consequences this time. He had previously speculated that his death and Blake's might be intertwined, a notion that now seems to hold true.

Vila's suggestion:

Vila was often perceived as the fool who was actually wise, a trait evident here. When the Scorpio is crashing, he suggests abandoning ship by teleporting down to the planet surface.

Though he may sometimes indulge in drunken self-pity, when under intense pressure, his mind sharpens.

Even Avon is compelled to acknowledge that Vila is correct.

Avon sets up his friends:

Avon uses his friends as bait to kill some gun runners and steal their flyer. Soolin realises what he has done and says she really could get quite annoyed about it, while Vila is used as the bungling comic relief one last time.

The tragedy of listening to Tarrant:

Despite the fact that Avon and Tarrant's relationship deteriorated somewhat after initially seeming like the two men were in harmony of sorts in the beginning of the third season, Avon seems to be quite willing to take Tarrant at his word here.

'He's sold us Avon, all of us, even you...' The Avon and Tarrant relationship has been rocky, but Avon seems so willing to believe everyone he cares about will ultimately betray him that he seemingly takes Tarrant's word without questioning him.

Avon loved Anna Grant and was betrayed. Why not Blake? But there is no doubt that believing Tarrant is Avon's biggest mistake.

Blake and Avon's final showdown:

'Have you betrayed us? Have YOU...betrayed ME?' With these immortal words, Avon confronts Blake, and it is one of the most gut wrenching and perfectly pitched scenes of all time.

Many viewers wondered if these two men would end up in some sort of a showdown and when it finally comes, it is so raw, so much of a heart-breaking tragedy, it almost seems surreal, as if we cannot quite take in what we are watching.

'Avon, I was waiting for YOU!' says Blake. And Avon shoots him.

Dayna's death triggers Vila into action:

As far back as 'Volcano', it was suggested that Vila had an eye for the pretty Dayna and was teased about this by Avon and Cally.

Tanith Lee's scripts for 'Sarcaophagus' and 'Sand' suggested that Dayna could be a little cruel and callous towards Vila, because his helplessness brought out her vindictive side.

And in 'Rescue', Vila even puts an arm around her, asking if she would prefer to cuddle up with those snakes on planet Terminal. She breaks away, asking if she can think about it.

Bearing this background in mind, it is interesting that Dayna is shot down as Vila tries to talk his way out of trouble with Arlen and it is the sight of Dayna gunned down which seems to trigger something in Vila.

There was always a braver, stronger, more cunning and clever man inside of Vila, waiting to come out. When Dayna is shot down, Vila takes this in, then disarms Arlen and knocks her out.

It is also interesting that he picks up Arlen's gun. Vila had never been the gunslinger type, yet here he grabs the gun, as if about to start shooting, only to be shot down.

Avon's state of shock:

Having killed Blake, Avon seems to go into a kind of state of shock. With Avon in his own little world, the others seemingly have no chance against the Federation troopers as they pour in.

It's only when everyone else is shot down that Avon finally seems to awaken to awareness of what is going on around him again.

The credits roll on gunfire:

The sirens stop and Avon looks up from staring down at Blake. Director Mary Ridge uses multiple camera shots, jumping closer and closer in on Paul Darrow's face. It's mesmerising work.

Paul Darrow has explained that upon finally realising Blake was not a traitor, but his one true friend, and that he has, ironically, killed him, he grins.

It is on this haunting freeze frame of Avon's face that the series goes to its end credits for the very last time. We hear gun fire and many fans were keen to note, the last shot we hear sounds like Avon's weapon firing.

As the credits come up for each actor and their character, it almost feels like the curtain call at the end of a Shakespearean tragedy on stage, with the cast members all taking their bows for an audience which has watched their show, watched their performances and experienced the emotion of the final tragic ending of the story.

THE

SLAVE COMPUTER'S MOST HUMBLE ASSESSMENT OF THE SITUATION:

10/10

REACTIONS TO 'BLAKE'

ONE: KEN DEEP

'Most of it wasn't on Earth, Tarrant...not what happened to me.'

An episode of this style should have taken place where 'Rescue' is placed, at the start of series D, maybe not the final moments, but everything prior to the flier's arrival at the base.

The tone of this story is the darkest of series D and it would have made this season more in line with the atmosphere of the previous series. Only a handful of occasions since series A have we revisited the dystopian universe so perfectly painted in the show's first year.

Between Boucher's script and Mary Ridge's direction the world building is excellent. If 'Rescue' shaped the series D universe closer to the style executed here we might have avoided the silliness seen in moments like the tricycle race seen in 'Stardrive'.

There are a number of ways that the show could have ended. We saw one possible version of that ending with 'Terminal'. 'Blake' offers a second, more definitive ending, of course.

But there was another possible ending hinted at within the very first episode 'The Way Back'. The pilot episode acts much like a prequel rather than a starting point where our principals are introduced.

I've maintained that Terry Nation's script for 'The Way Back' sets the ending up for one that would have resembled the finale of *The Prisoner*.

This possible ending is teased throughout series A as the character of Blake reminds us that his memory has been erased and that nearly the same events have reoccurred. I love this idea, even if it is too close to Patrick McGoohan's iconic finale.

Chris Boucher made the best ending he could, not once but twice, but avoided this circular finish even though Gareth Thomas returned for both series ending occasions when asked.

As attractive as the circular ending is, the final moments of 'Blake' were shocking and definitive.

In addition to leaving the audience aghast, Boucher avoids the obvious *Prisoner* comparison creating an iconic ending worthy of this influential iconic show.

REACTIONS TO 'BLAKE'

TWO: ADRIAN SHERLOCK

'Avon, I was waiting for you!'

This may sound like a silly thing to say about a TV show, because it is only a TV show, but the series ending had such an effect on me as a teenager that I struggled for years to really continue being a fan of the series. Looking back, now, I believe it was a form of unresolved grief.

I know it is silly because they are just fictional characters, but they got under people's skin. They got into my heart and the final ending scarred me and shocked me in ways that I struggled to understand at the time. No doubt this happened for many other young viewers as well.

As an older adult, I've finally been able to release the emotion I couldn't as a youngster. I had to heal, in a way, before I could truly enjoy this show again. It sounds crazy to say this about a television series, but that was the impact of *Blake's 7*. It is absurd, but it literally feels like witnessing a tragedy.

Avon's reaction to the sight of Blake is incredibly powerful. 'Have YOU betrayed ME?' It's as if he believed in one thing being certain, that Blake was incorruptible and when he thinks it's happened, it breaks him. The idea that Blake has betrayed him just simply breaks him.

Paul Darrow is so good here; he nails the emotion completely. He could be hammy in season four, or series D as it was known at the BBC, but in this very last episode, his acting was masterful.

Everything worked in the final episode and that's why it had such an amazing impact.

After watching 'Terminal' again, it struck me that we heard Blake was dead, it was implied Servalan may have died, we heard Zen die and saw Liberator blown up, but it was still very much in line with Terry Nation's beloved writing axiom 'never kill anything off.'

But when we get to 'Blake', there is a sense of a production team who are thinking, 'this time we're doing the job *properly*! This time we are going to kill this show once and for all!'

Blowing up Xenon base, crashing Scorpio, Tarrant appearing to die plunging through the floor, and then Blake revealed to be actually alive, Tarrant is actually alive, and then we kill Blake again only this time we see it so there's no doubt, we kill Tarrant again, properly this time and kill everyone else, it's like 'last time you didn't die properly so this time we're going to kick your corpse and dance on your grave to really make sure you're dead!'

I personally like to tell myself they are still alive, apart from Blake, just concussed or wounded or something for the short term. I'm just an eternal optimist.

But the way the massacre of our rebel heroes mirrors the massacre of the rebels which Blake witnesses in 'The Way Back' is so perfect and fitting, it seems impossible to argue that this wasn't exactly the right ending, painful though it may be to accept.

I think I've force fed myself enough viewings of the series recently to finally get over the pain of how it all ended and accept that I do actually love this show, despite the way it hurt me as a youngster.

But whose show was it? Certainly Blake looms large over it all, even in absentia. Vila might be my favourite character of the lot, in a way, a kind of audience identification figure who is more down to Earth than the others. Perhaps a story is waiting to be written, telling it all again from his perspective.

While it's either Blake or Avon's show, Vila is the other guy who runs through the whole thing and in many ways is a very relatable antihero. Many fans loved how they hinted he was much more clever and capable than the other crew members realised.

Of course, he had to screw up at times, for plot purposes, but he had the potential to be the star in his own way. Maybe that would've made the show too much like another *Doctor Who*, with a funny tech guy as the lead.

But Chris Boucher did show us who Vila was in 'City at the Edge of the World' and at the very end of the final episode, it's Vila who shows the most cunning as he approaches Arlen.

I like to believe Vila survived the end of the

series and is having further misadventures in space and time to this day. Hell, I want to believe they all survived!

REACTIONS TO 'BLAKE'

THREE: ANDREW SAUNDERS

Ruminations on 'Blake'.

This episode had been slated as the final episode. It was no closed secret, but everyone continued on regardless.

But it's virtually impossible to review this story without a reflection... and some background

THE BACKGROUND:

The production crew spent virtually the entire of season four, negotiating to get Gareth Back. He wanted nothing more to do with the series, and it took a lot of negotiating to get him back, even for one episode.

Reluctantly, he finally agreed, but wanted a major script rewrite, so he reached out to Paul and Michael.

Michael was working on Agatha Christie productions and was keeping busy otherwise. Paul, being an author, agreed to help.

Behind the scenes, they worked with the Script. They both wanted no credit. Who would?

The only reason I knew because they both agreed to have this fact published in *Horizon Magazine - The official Magazine of Blake's 7*.

A REFLECTION:

The entire of Season Four was a gradual wind down to the inevitable. After the destruction of The Liberator, fans were mixed on the introduction of Scorpio, and having a 'Home Base'.

During the season, fans expressed mixed feelings about the series, and some even offered to take over to extend it. In fact, there have been at least seven attempts to revitalise the series since, all to no fruition.

Fast forward to today, and fans still petition to revitalise the series, and there has been books, audios and even scripts drawn up.

But it has been hard for any production, due to the sad loss of the most revered cast: Gareth, Jaqueline, David (Gan) and of course, the late Paul.

To start the series again, it would have to go through a complete recast. Whilst Michael and Josette still stay in touch of the fans, Michael is now semi-retired. Steven moved on and didn't look back.

TERRY NATION: A LEGACY

BY ANDREW SAUNDERS

Without Terry, we wouldn't have Blake's 7. And if he had his way, it would have kept running.

He created the series and was personally involved in gathering the cast and crew of the series. He was extremely involved and invested in the series and sought out Chris Boucher as a great script editor.

There isn't a member of the cast and crew who didn't speak highly of Terry, and many attended his funeral, out of respect.

He was involved everywhere. And by everywhere, I mean from those you see, to those you never see. Costumes, Special Effects, lighting, sound, score, make up, hair stylists, cameras, and Emergency services.

True, he is better known for creating The Daleks, but Blake's 7 still remains one of his proudest legacies.

May his legacy last a lifetime!

So, is this a story review? Not really. In spite of a massive rewrite by both Paul and Gareth, it's still not a fan favourite, nor a popular story. The story itself has a flimsy pretext and the final scene on reflection is almost surreal, like it's not really happening.

Frankly, it's easy to see how many fans have dismissed this episode as being 'Canon', then coming up with a variety of ways that none of the cast were actually killed - including Terry Nation, who was involved in the book story 'Afterlife', where he brought back his three favourites: Avon, Vila and Orac.

WHAT NOW?

Who really knows? As mentioned before. There have (ironically) been at least seven attempts to bring the series back, including an Audio Series: many books - written by fans, cast members and script writers; scripts, pre productions, funding and a lot of research.

Many fans see the *Star Trek Series: Deep Space Nine*, as the closest we've had to the series yet. And it's true that both Rick Berman and Michael Piller knew about the series.

Whether this had any influence in the script is anyone's guess, but still, parallels have been cited.

But you could also say that about *Babylon 5*. In fact, creator J. Michael Straczynski is a self-confessed fan of *Blake's 7* and has often commented on his fondness for the character of Kerr Avon, even posting on social media about the passing of Paul Darrow.

The legacy of *Blake's 7* is that it still continues to influence the pop culture of science fiction until today.

And long may it stay in our consciousness.

Vila! Bring me up!

VHS VIDEO AND DVD SET RELEASES

The initial home video release of Blake's 7 made its debut in UK shops in September 1985. Titled *The Beginning*, it featured a heavily edited two-hour compilation of the first four episodes from the first series.

The Beginning was released on VHS (BBCV2000) and Betamax (BBCB2000) formats, featuring cover art by Tony Geddes. It includes Episode 1: 'The Way Back', Episode 2: 'Space Fall', Episode 3: 'Cygnus Alpha', and Episode 4: 'Time Squad'.

There were three subsequent compilations called *Duel, Orac*, and *The Aftermath*.

They serve as a pleasant reminder of the sheer excitement of *Blake's 7* and the compelling story arcs it boasted during its time.

However, in 'The Way Back', the editing is quite extensive, making it appear as though Blake was arrested simply for venturing outside the city.

The trial was omitted, but the sentencing was included. The subplot involving his lawyer was dropped, but in the 'Space Fall' section, Raiker still accuses Blake of molestation, to which Blake vehemently denies any guilt. So, while condensed, the essence of the subplot remains present.

The adult content of the first two episodes has been toned down and subplots not focused on the main characters have been removed.

The BBC eventually made the decision to cater to a younger audience, including children, and retroactively toned down the fact that Blake was accused of moral misconduct against minors.

Despite the somewhat poor picture and audio quality in those early VHS days, watching three or four episodes together was a lot of fun and helped maintain the series' popularity.

Duel features 'Seek Locate Destroy', 'Duel' and 'Project Avalon'. To fit the two-hour run time, these episodes are only reduced by approximately ten minutes, including the title sequences.

Orac features 'Deliverance', 'Orac' and season two premiere 'Redemption'. These episodes have been reduced by approximately ten minutes, including title sequences, to fit the two-hour runtime, just like the previous release.

These first three episodes provide us with ten out of the first fourteen episodes by Terry Nation, albeit in a condensed form. The remaining four episodes, namely 'The Web', 'Mission to Destiny', 'Bounty', and 'Breakdown', are the closest to being stand-alone stories. This highlights the emphasis on the story arc aspect.

'Aftermath', 'Power Play', and 'Sarcophagus' comprise the final VHS telemovie-style edition released in the years following the conclusion of the series, titled *The Aftermath*. Without the context of Star One, viewers who only had the VHS compilation videos would likely assume that Gan went missing, just like Blake and Jenna.

It does avoid the issue of Brian Croucher replacing Stephen Greif as Travis.

The alien war with the Federation would

have been rather out of left field, too, although the back cover text explains the aliens were from Andromeda and it describes Star One as the Federation's power base.

With the inclusion of the Sarcophagus as the final part, casual viewers would have been led to assume that the new line-up was embarking on new adventures at the end, and that would be the end of it.

However, with Avon kissing Dayna and Cally in these episodes, the final VHS movie seems to conclude on a happy note for Avon. He is now in charge of the ship he desired and finally free.

The opening credits might be the biggest curiosity. The combination of 'The Aftermath' by Terry Nation and Tanith Lee is probably one that few people ever expected to see.

In October 1986, the first compilation appeared exclusively on Laserdisc format in Japan. It was published by the Pony Canyon label.

In April 1990, *The Beginning* was re-

released on VHS (BBCV4236) with a PG certification now included on the video sleeve. The following year, BBC Video made a commitment to release all 52 episodes of *Blake's 7* (virtually) complete and unedited on VHS.

By the time the complete VHS release was done, the digital era was beginning and soon the DVD boxed sets would be planned. These were released as four complete season boxed sets early in the early 2000s.

A REBOOT OR A SEQUEL REVIVAL?

There have been many attempts to revive *Blake's 7* which have failed to produce a TV show or movie so far. But what type of revival would we really like to see?

Reboots are actually a fairly awful idea and I have no idea why people keep talking about them. Is it possible to name a handful of reboots that have worked? There have been one or two where the use of character names from the old series was almost pointless because there was little or no comparison.

The best idea is probably a revival of sorts, set years later, with new characters who continue on in the same universe as the original show being revived.

This is why *Doctor Who* worked in 2005. No one tried to suggest that actor Christopher Eccleston was the First Doctor, he was clearly announced as the Ninth from the outset, acknowledging the classic series as the backstory to the new series.

If *Blake's 7* came back, it would and should be a new group of freedom fighters who simply fight in the same spirit as their hero, the legendary Blake, much in the same way Blake's crew kept on fighting in the third and fourth season in his absence.

All you would need is a batch of merry men and women (because it was Robin Hood in space, despite Terry Nation's cool-sounding comments to the media that he was inspired by *The Dirty Dozen*) and evil government types and a decent spaceship. The leader of the rebels has heard the tales of Blake's exploits, and it gives him the idea of fighting the oppressors.

It might be nice to have a revival of *Blake's 7* with new characters who are scripted in a manner reminiscent of the original, just not having two new actors calling themselves Avon and Vila. The originals were perfectly cast and should probably be left alone.

With so many futuristic names in the *Blake's 7* universe to choose from, we could have a group of seven with names like Dev, Arko, Nova and Glyn and probably a blonde woman named Tarrant (since we had Dev,

Del and Deeta Tarrants in the series) and possibly add a Rebec and it would feel authentic without needing to be exactly the same names.

It might be fun to pop in someone called Avon who says, 'no relation' and gets bumped off in the first episode, just put in as a red herring.

The notion from the first season that 'Blake is becoming a legend' is something of a way into this idea, too. Legends need never appear, like in the play *Waiting for Godot*. Characters can be like knights of God on a Holy Crusade without God actually showing up, just acting in His name.

The legend of Blake could become the inspiration, without needing to be seen. But there could be a great device where someone in the team reads a little extract from a book about the legend of Blake, a book which the Federation has outlawed and wants all copies destroyed.

We could even have someone who was raised to know them since childhood and can recite the legendary tales of Blake from memory, so it survives the tyranny of the

Federation thanks to a revival of the oral tradition. The possibilities are endless.

Meanwhile, the series has been the subject of audio dramas such as Barry Letts scripted *The Sevenfold Crown* and *The Syndeton Experiment,* Silver Bullet Productions audio plays *The Mark of Kane* and *The Logic of Empire,* an audio drama by Ben Aaronovitch for B7 Media and a *Blake's 7* audio revival by Big Finish Productions.

There was also a sequel novel called 'Afterlife' by Tony Attwood as well as original novels by Paul Darrow and a wealth of fan fiction dealing with what might have happened after the events of the final episode on Gauda Prime.

What will the future bring? Will the series ever become a TV viewing experience again? *Doctor Who* was revived, perhaps *Blake's 7* will be as well, some day. In a big galaxy, anything is possible.

VINDICTUS

Enjoy a brand new era of *Blake's 7* adventure. *Vindictus* by Neil Shearer and Louella Richardson picks up the *Blake's 7* gauntlet and takes off into a whole new galaxy of excitement.

Vindictus is a fan created not for profit sci fi series. *Vindictus* is a brand new science fiction series written by two science fiction fans, Louella Richardson and Neil Shearer following the adventures of a group of disparate outcasts starting a fresh resistance against the tyrannical Federation.

Decades after the death of Roj Blake, the Federation has located Orac. This results in a chain of events that brings together a group of disparate outcasts. They start a fresh resistance under a young leader with a strong tie to the past.

Enjoy a brand new era of *Blake's 7* adventure! Vindictus by Neil Shearer and Louella Richardson picks up the Blake's 7 gauntlet and takes off into a whole new galaxy of excitement.

GUEST CONTRIBUTORS

KEN DEEP

Ken Deep has been active in organized *Doctor Who* fandom for over 40 years.

The co-host of *Doctor Who: Podshock*, he became an international pioneer of new media in 2005 as one of the world's first podcasters.

He is currently the showrunner of the annual Long Island Doctor Who convention.

A contributor to the book *A World of Demons: The Villains of Doctor Who* and editor of *The Companions of Doctor Who*.

RUSSELL DEVLIN

Russell Devlin used to contribute to and edit things for Fanclub newsletters back in the heyday for *Doctor Who*, *Blakes 7*, *Hitchers & Goon Club*, and more recently for his friend Jeff Kelley's podcasts *Coffee with Jeff & Celluloid Days*.

A gifted animator and director, Russell also makes animated short film with his fan production company Black Maria, often based on classic comics or TV series.

ANDREW SAUNDERS

(DUGGAN)

Andrew Saunders is a talented singer and photographer with a long history of passionate involvement in fan clubs and fan writing and editing.

He has met many of the stars of *Blake's 7*, *Doctor Who* and more.

He was part of a spin-off fanzine called "Vila-world" in which Vila got to go off and live life in another dimension of reality.

ABOUT THE AUTHOR

Born in 1966, Adrian Sherlock grew up in working class Corio, in the Australian city of Geelong. He dreamed of writing, acting and film making. He got his first break in 1986, doing local theatre work before finding an agent in 1988. After a brief career in minor work in film and television, Adrian shifted into local theatre and studied to become a writer and teacher.

In 1999 he produced and performed in an independent television series called Damon Dark, which screened on Community TV (Channel 31) in Melbourne.

YouTube brought him back to film making and acting in 2006 when he helped launch web series such as Damon Dark and Vincent Kosmos.

In 2012, he performed a one-man stage show in Geelong, based on his Damon Dark UFO hunter character.

Adrian Sherlock is also a writer, whose first published novel was a tie-in to the *Doctor Who television* series, titled Lethbridge-

Stewart: The New Unusual and published by Candy Jar Books.

He has a journalism degree and an MA in writing and has written several viewer's guidebooks about classic British TV series which inspired him.

One last note:

Sincere gratitude for your purchase. If you enjoyed reading this viewer's guide, *please consider leaving a review, or a star rating,* where you purchased this edition!

Printed in Great Britain
by Amazon

46332616R00126